REACHING FOR

HEALING

REACHING FOR
HEALING

Closing the gap between experience and expectation

Marcus Tutt

Mango Press 2017

ISBN 978-1-326-60359-5

First Printing: 2017

Mango Press

Norwich, UK

DEDICATION

To my wonderful wife and
two lovely daughters.

CONTENTS

ACKNOWLEDGEMENTS

I would like to thank everyone who helped me proofread this book. Without all of your hard work, I would not have been able to get it into a readable state, so thank you so much. Any remaining errors are, of course, down to me and hopefully won't detract too much from the material that I want to share with you.

PREFACE

I cannot pinpoint the exact time or date when the penny dropped for me, but I know there was a moment when it did. It was not just that God *wanted* to heal people supernaturally but that he *would*. I knew it with more certainty than I knew almost anything else. A solid conviction had appeared like a cube of steel in my heart. It was heavy, real, tangible, and totally un-squashable.

It all happened so quickly, I'm not sure which came first— the reasoning or the conviction. The argument could have led to the conclusion, or the conviction could have constructed its own justification. In any case, my thinking went like this: "If the author of the Bible didn't realise the massive expectation that they were raising for supernatural healing in the minds of future readers, then they were a pretty poor communicator."

Now, I believe the Bible to be not just the work of many people over many hundreds of years, but fully inspired and "breathed out" by God. And since God (who is *the* communicator) is the author, there is simply no way that he is unaware of the impression that his book gives: namely, that Christians will see lots and lots of miraculous healings. I certainly cannot imagine him saying, "Oh, yes, now you come to mention it, it does sort of come across like that, doesn't it?"

It wasn't so much that any particular passage persuaded me, but that the Bible as a whole, from Genesis to Revelation, spoke with one voice on the matter. A single drop of water falling on your nose doesn't necessarily mean rain. After all, it could have been blown from a waterlogged leaf on a nearby tree, but when you are soaked from head to toe and all around you puddles are filling up fast, it's hard to come to any other conclusion than that the heavens have opened. Previously, I had spent time looking at individual passages, but when I stepped back and considered the Bible as a whole, especially the New Testament, there was really only one conclusion: God did heal then, and he will heal now.

At the time, God was encouraging our church to "reach for fruit". With the eye of faith we could see all kinds of fruit that was there for the taking, if only we would reach out for it. We decided, therefore, to make "Reaching for Fruit" the title of the next year's preaching series. It would have three strands, and I was thrilled when it was agreed that my part would be called "Reaching for Fruit in Supernatural Healing".

My original plan was to break it up into three parts and look at healing in the gospels, healing in Acts, and healing in the Old Testament. In the end, it took a year to go through the first two, so the last would have to wait for another time. This book is the product of that year of study, prayer, and preaching. It is based on the material I preached, and through it I invite you to join us in reaching for fruit in supernatural healing.

At the end of each chapter I have included a few questions for personal reflection or group discussion. They are intended to help you think about what you have read and how to apply it to your life. I hope you find them helpful.

PART I
THE HEALING POWER OF JESUS
IN THE GOSPELS

INTRODUCTION TO PART I

When I first began to seriously seek God for breakthrough in supernatural healing, I had no clear theology of healing or indeed much practical experience with it. I decided, therefore, to study some of the numerous accounts of healing in the Bible and share what I found with the church through our next preaching series.

Even one sermon on healing seemed like a daunting task, so I had no idea how I would preach a dozen times on the subject. Would the Bible really have that much to say about it? Would people get tired of hearing the same thing?

The gospels seemed like a good place to start, so I went through Matthew's gospel and picked out all the healing miracles. To my surprise, I discovered that Matthew had done much of the hard work for me by grouping several of Jesus' healing miracles together into a couple of chapters. I decided, therefore, simply to preach through them one healing miracle at a time and discovered as I did so that each one highlighted a key aspect of healing that God wanted to teach us.

The first chapter in Part I of this book takes an overview of Matthew 8 and 9 and aims to show just how much Jesus loved to heal. The following chapters highlight Jesus' authority to heal, the link between healing and the cross, and the central place of healing in the proclamation of the gospel. Part I finishes with a look at the healing power of touch.

1. THE EXPECTATION OF HEALING

"Jesus went through all the towns and villages,
teaching in their synagogues, preaching the good news of the
kingdom and healing every disease and every affliction."
Matthew 9:35

SEEING THE WOOD FOR THE TREES

In 1999 scientists discovered signs of an ancient civilisation in a
region that straddles the border between Brazil and Bolivia.
The people walking on the ground had missed the significance
of the bumps and dips, but from the air, as the rain forest was
cut down, large scale patterns became apparent. Vast ditches
and enclosures testified to the existence of a previously
unknown civilisation in the Amazon basin.

Sometimes we can get so close to a passage of scripture,
and examine it in such detail, that we fail to see the bigger
picture and, as the expression goes, we "can't see the wood for
the trees". In the same way, it is possible to read a story of
Jesus healing someone and see it as a one-off: a special or
unusual event. We can quickly move on to another passage and
forget all about healing. But as we pull back from the Bible and

gain altitude, a pattern emerges: an ancient forest of supernatural activity that can no longer be ignored.

Matthew, one of Jesus' disciples, saw this and in order to bring it to our attention collected many of the healing miracles of Jesus together in his gospel. In chapters 8 and 9 he describes how Jesus healed one person after another and then in chapter 10 recalled how Jesus sent out his disciples to do the same.

First, a man with leprosy comes to Jesus and is made clean (Matthew 8:1–5). Then Jesus heals a centurion's servant of paralysis (Matthew 8:5–10, 13) and Peter's mother-in-law of a fever (Matthew 8:14–15). He goes on to heal many more people and cast out demons (Matthew 8:16–17) fulfilling, we are told, what was spoken about him through the prophet Isaiah. After talking about the cost of following him, and calming a storm, Jesus casts out demons from two extremely strong and violent men (Matthew 8:28–34), and all that is just for starters.

Next, a paralysed man is lowered down through the roof (Matthew 9:1–8) to be healed by Jesus in what becomes a spectacular demonstration of his power to forgive sins. Jesus calls Matthew to follow him (Matthew 9:9–14), talks about fasting (Matthew 9:14–17), then responds to the heartfelt plea of a father to raise his little girl from the dead. On the way, a woman is instantly healed as she reaches through the crowd to touch Jesus' robe (Matthew 9:18–26). Finally, Jesus heals two blind men and someone unable to speak (Matthew 9:27–34). Can you imagine the excitement, wonder, and amazement that must have spread like wildfire around the region? No wonder crowds flocked to Jesus and followed him everywhere he went.

Chapter 9 ends with a summary of Jesus' ministry and his desire to multiply it:

> Jesus went through all the towns and villages, teaching in their synagogues, preaching the good news of the kingdom and healing every disease and sickness. When

> he saw the crowds, he had compassion on them, because they were harassed and helpless, like sheep without a shepherd. Then he said to his disciples, "The harvest is plentiful but the workers are few. Ask the Lord of the harvest, therefore, to send out workers into his harvest field." (Matthew 9:35–38)

Then, at the start of chapter 10, Jesus sends out the twelve to do what he has just been doing:

> He called his twelve disciples to him and gave them authority to drive out evil spirits and to heal every disease and sickness … These twelve Jesus sent out with the following instructions: … Heal the sick, raise the dead, cleanse those who have leprosy, drive out demons. (Matthew 10:1–8)

After reading these chapters, it is impossible to miss the central place that healing played in Jesus' ministry. That would be like reading Shakespeare's biography and not noticing that he wrote plays!

At the risk of stating the obvious, it's clear from these accounts that Jesus healed a lot of people: a man with leprosy, a centurion's servant, Peter's mother-in-law, a paralysed man, a dead girl, a woman subject to bleeding, two blind men, and a mute; plus many, many more people from every disease and sickness.

Have you ever played the Word Association game? You start with a word like "cat", then your opponent has to say a word semantically related to it, like "dog", but they are not allowed to hesitate. Usually it's best just to trust the synaptic connections in your brain and say the first word that comes into your head. If I say "eggs", your instant reaction might be something like "bacon". Let's try it.

As you read each of the following words, simply say the first thing that comes into your head: Bread, Salt, Green, Jesus.

Now, I wonder if you went out onto the streets and played that game with passers-by, what words would they come back with in response to "Jesus"? They might say "teacher" or "prophet" or "charlatan" or "sandals" or, maybe even, "forgiving". What about the people in your church? What would they say? You might expect them to be generally more positive and answer "Saviour" or "Lord". What about you? What did you say?

Now here is the thing: I bet if you asked the people who heard about Jesus during the three years of his public ministry, many would immediately say "healer" or "miracles". Wouldn't it be great to see Jesus' name once again intimately associated with supernatural power and healing?

WHY DOES JESUS HEAL?

When someone does something, it's often helpful to consider their motive and ask why they are acting in a certain way. Establishing the motive behind an action tells you a lot about a person—whether they are likely to do it again and in what circumstances—so let's consider why Jesus spends so much time healing people.

Firstly, *Jesus heals in response to human need*. When the leper says "Lord if you are willing, make me clean" (Matthew 8:2), it turns out that Jesus is willing. When a centurion tells him "Lord my servant lies at home paralysed and in terrible suffering", Jesus' immediate response is "I will come and heal him" (Matthew 8:7). As soon as a sick woman touches Jesus in faith, power goes out from him, and she is healed (Matthew 9:22). It seems that healing is such an integral part of him that someone can get healed without him knowing who it was! Finally, when two blind men cry out to Jesus, "Have mercy on us" (Matthew 9:27) he does, and heals them both.

Secondly, *Jesus heals to show who he is*. Healing is an identifying mark of the Messiah. Isaiah prophesied that he would "take up our infirmities and carry our diseases"

8

(Matthew 8:17; Isaiah 53:4). When John the Baptist is languishing in prison, he seeks reassurance that Jesus is the promised Saviour. Jesus sends John's disciples back to report what they have seen and heard: "the blind receive their sight and the lame walk, lepers are cleansed and the deaf hear, and the dead are raised up" (Matthew 11:4, 5). When Jesus is explaining to his disciples that he is one with the Father, he says in effect, "At least believe on the evidence of the miracles!" (John 14:11).

Thirdly, by his miraculous healings *Jesus showcases the coming kingdom of God.* He sent his twelve disciples out to preach "The kingdom of heaven is at hand" (Matthew 10:7) and to prove it by healing the sick. Healing is such a central part of the kingdom of God that each time we pray "your kingdom come" in the Lord's Prayer it should remind us to pray for healing.

Fourthly, *Jesus heals to authenticate his claim to be able to forgive sins.* After pronouncing a paralytic's sins forgiven, Jesus tells him to get up (Matthew 9:6). As the man does so, the Scribes' charge of blasphemy falls to the ground.

So Jesus heals out of compassion to demonstrate the kingdom, to show who he is, and to authenticate his authority to forgive sins, but I want to drive home the significance of all this even further: *Jesus is the full revelation of who God is.* If you have seen him, you have seen the Father. This is a result of their unity. If you encounter Jesus or hear about Jesus or read about Jesus, you are encountering, hearing, or reading about God. The writer to the Hebrews tells us that "in these last days [God the Father] has spoken to us by his Son" (Hebrews 1:2). The fact, therefore, that Jesus loves to heal and does so at every opportunity, tells us in the clearest possible way that God is in the business of making people well.

After reading these passages, no one can say that God is reticent to heal people. It seems to me that if I read the gospels and come to any conclusion other than that God is a healer, intent upon healing people from deafness, blindness, skin conditions, paralysis, and all other diseases and sicknesses, then on this matter at least, I might as well be reading the Beano comic for all the revelation I'd be getting from them. How many more people does Jesus have to heal to get it through to us?

JESUS SENDS US OUT TO HEAL

So far we have been looking at the healing ministry of Jesus. It's always good to focus on Jesus and look to him (Hebrews 12:2). He is the only begotten Son of God who is one with the Father and who was sent as the unique, once for all, sacrifice for our sin. However, we might think that it's one thing for Jesus to heal, but quite another for you and I to do likewise. Jesus is sinless, we are sinful; he is omnipotent, we are weak and frail. Yet at the beginning of chapter 10, after the healing bonanza of the last two chapters, Jesus sends out his twelve disciples to continue the good work he has started.

Whilst acknowledging this fact, we might be tempted to respond, "Oh, but the Twelve were special." But then what about the seventy two? Didn't he send them ahead of him into every town with instructions to "Heal the sick" (Luke 10:9)? Were they special too? How many special cases can there be?

What about Jesus' statement that "these signs will accompany those who believe ... they will place their hands on sick people and they will get well" (Mark 16:18)? If you are concerned that the ending of Mark's gospel is not in the earliest manuscripts then consider the ending of Matthew's gospel. There Jesus tells his disciples to make more disciples. What does that entail? Well, he defined it as "teaching them to obey everything I have commanded you" (Matthew 28:20). What did Jesus keep telling his disciples to do? "Heal the sick" (Matthew 10:8). Then in Acts we see believers like Stephen, Philip, Paul, and Barnabas doing just that, and of course, in the New Testament letters, we see the Holy Spirit distributing gifts of healings among the churches (1 Corinthians 12:9; 12:28).

We need to jettison any residual Old Covenant thinking and recognise the significance of the times we are living in. Under the Old Covenant, God generally did special things through special people on special occasions. Now, under the New Covenant, he has poured out his Spirit on all people and there is to be an abundance of Holy Spirit activity—an abundance of God doing what he loves to do through those he loves. These are special times, and we are all special people with a special task to do. When Jesus healed people, he didn't turn to camera and say, "Don't try this at home." Rather, he turned to his disciples and said, "Now it's your turn!"

LIVING IN THE GAP

Having said all that though, the real reason why many of us struggle with the idea of supernatural healing is not to do with understanding the theology of the Old and New Covenants. Let me be frank: my problem is not with understanding the theology but with my experience. My personal experience tells me that people don't tend to get miraculously healed—at least, not instantly, there and then, in the name of Jesus. I usually see people getting sick and staying sick. If I look at my current experience, I could easily deduce that healing is highly exceptional in Christianity. Most of the time it seems God either can't or won't heal people, and occasionally, just once in a while for reasons only known to himself, in an almost out of character way, he heals someone. It certainly does not look to me like this is one of his key strategies for extending his kingdom, or his normal way of working. In my experience, healing is the exception not the rule.

Yet, in the Bible, haven't we just seen quite the opposite: healing after healing, miracle after miracle? The exception seems to be people not getting healed. There is the odd hint that occasionally, maybe, not everyone was always walking around in full health, free from sickness. But come on, the fact that Timothy had tummy trouble (1 Timothy 5:23) doesn't even begin to overturn the weight of biblical testimony piling up and giving me a massive expectation for supernatural healing. Jesus and his disciples healed the sick and raised the dead yet we say, "Wait a minute; Timmy's got a dicky tummy. That changes everything!" No. It changes nothing. Healing is clearly and overwhelmingly presented in the Bible as the norm, and surely that, not our current or past experience, should govern our expectation.

It can be very sobering to recognise the gulf that lies between our current experience and the biblical picture, and to let ourselves be shocked by the size of that gap. Sometimes we are embarrassed or confused by it so we turn away, but I want to face it down and look this discrepancy in the eye. If I wrote a book about the last ten years of my life, it would not be filled with the supernatural activity I find in the book of Acts. In fact, the two would be glaringly different in content. It just doesn't line up, and that's painfully hard to live with, so what should I do?

The temptation, as we look into this gulf, is to try to pull the Bible into line with our experience. One way of doing that is to make the few exceptions where someone is not healed (Galatians 4:14; 1 Timothy 5:23; 2 Timothy 4:20; Philippians 2:27) the rule. Going a step further, some end up saying that God doesn't heal today and that he began to back off healing even while the apostles were still alive. This cessationism, as it's called, is in many ways quite an attractive position to take. A lack of current miracles can be a very persuasive hermeneutic, and drawing a line under miracles after the Bible was written neatly explains why some of us don't see many now. The problem for me though is that this version of events is not supported by the Bible itself.

Another approach for some is to consider the Bible to be full of myths and legends: nothing more than rumours and hearsay. Though this liberalism may concede that the Bible is a very interesting and insightful book, it is nevertheless still a completely human work. Sometimes a little chronological snobbery can creep in where people in the past are seen as less perceptive and intelligent than us. We think that because they didn't have our scientific knowledge they believed any old wives tales that were doing the rounds. When I read the Bible, however, I find people doubting and investigating miracles in much the same way as we might do today (John 9:8–10, 18–21).

Though there is a lot of discussion and debate around both cessationism and liberalism, I expect a few more miracles would go a long way in arguing the case that healing is, indeed, for today. What's more, the truth of the matter is that the Bible isn't going to budge. It says what it says, and no matter how people try to interpret it, it seems plain to me that it raises a massive, sky-high expectation for the miraculous. No, we can't move God's word, so there is only one other possibility if this gap is to close: our experience is going to have to change.

Our experience needs to be pulled into line with our biblical expectation, and that happens by a little thing that crops up quite a lot in the Bible. It's something that God really loves, and it thrives in gaps like this. It is called faith, and just like fish live in water, faith thrives in the ecological niche between our experience and our expectation. It's less interested in why these two things do not line up and more interested in getting them to line up.

This is going to sound strange at first, but hear me out. When we have a biblical expectation, faith can actually rise even when we don't see people getting healed. Why? Because experience is moving away from the testimony of God's word, and that cannot continue for long. In this sense, true faith is like a spring. The more it is extended between God's word and our current experience, the more force it exerts, until in the end, experience is pulled back into line.

DAM BUSTERS

Jesus was massively motivated to heal the sick. He was equally determined that his disciples should follow in his footsteps and move in miracles too. Over the years there have been seismic shifts in large sections of Christianity, opening up barren canyons between what the Bible promises and what we actually practice. It is time for a tectonic realigning of our experience with the word of God as we step out in faith to heal the sick.

Let me end this chapter with a prophetic picture a friend of mine shared with me. As we read the Bible and respond with faith, it's like water rising behind a dam. The dam is made of past experience, anti-supernaturalism, scepticism, false teaching, and plain old unbelief. On the other side of the dam is a dry, parched valley where people are dying, both physically and spiritually. There are dried up river beds of past outpourings but very little water. As we take God's word seriously, the pressure builds, and cracks start to appear in the dam. One day it will break, and the trickle will turn into a torrent. We don't know all the whys and wherefores behind the events of our lives, but we have been told what we must do: trust, pray, and step out to heal the sick.

QUESTIONS

1) What stories of supernatural healing have you experienced or heard about?

   Are there any you recall from the Old Testament? Take a look at some of the following: Genesis 20:17–18; 1 Kings 13:4–6; 17:17–24; 2 Kings 4:18–37; 5:1–14; Numbers 21:4–9. Why do you think God healed those people?

2) Have you noticed a gap between what the Bible seems to say and your actual experience? Think about some specific examples if you can.

3) In what ways have you sought to reconcile what you read in the Bible with your current experience? How helpful, fruitful, and true to the Bible have they been?

2. THE AUTHORITY FOR HEALING

"... only say the word,
and my servant will be healed"
Matthew 8:8

THEORY AND PRACTICE

Right now, I am trying to learn New Testament Greek. It's a bit of an uphill struggle, but I am making progress. One of the things I have noticed about learning a language is that, like many other things, there are two aspects to it: the theory and the practice. I read a chapter of my text book and learn the theory, but when I come to apply it and do some real translation, I find there is another learning process going on. The theory gets me so far, but to read Greek fluently and put into practice what I have learned requires more on the job learning. I need to know the theory to get anywhere at all, but I won't learn the language unless I do tons of real "roll-your-sleeves-up" translation.

Imagine how far you would get if you tried to learn to drive just by reading the theory. You might study the mechanics of the engine and the chemistry of the petrol. You might learn the Highway Code inside out and how many millimetres to put the accelerator down when going 30mph up a 10% incline in third gear, but how well would you drive when getting into the car for the first time? In all probability, not very successfully. To get anywhere safely, another learning process needs to kick in as you put into practice what you know in theory.

I believe the same is true of biblical truth in general and supernatural healing in particular. We should not just be hearers of God's word, but doers. The Bible is to be lived not just studied. It cannot be correctly analysed in isolation from the faithful and persistent practice of what it actually says.

In the West, we currently have a culture of educating people in theory for years before they get their hands dirty with practice. This wasn't always the case. In the past, vocational training and apprenticeships placed much more emphasis on learning while doing, usually alongside an expert. They would not show you how to make a barrel by drawing on a whiteboard, but would show you how to make a barrel by making a barrel. Now, of course, things have moved on. Many skills like building jet engines are highly technical and require lots of theory. I'm still struck, however, by the way Jesus taught his disciples; it was very practical.

It also seems to me that when Jesus ascended, he did not just leave us with a book, but sent the Holy Spirit to guide, counsel, and train us. I do not, of course, want to undermine in any way the role of God's written word, but rather highlight the fact that we also have the Holy Spirit in us. It's the Holy Spirit who helps us understand and put into practice God's word every second of the day, and in fact we will not truly understand God's words until we learn to apply them. Jesus said that the wise man not only hears his words, but puts them into practice, and James points out that we deceive ourselves if we just listen without acting (Matthew 27:24–27; James 1:22).

As we look at what God says about healing, there may be many things we do not understand. Why didn't so and so get healed? How come that big shot healing evangelist doesn't empty all the hospitals? How will I know if God wants to heal someone in particular? These are not bad questions to ask, and God's word does help us with them. However, as in many other areas of God's word, we will at some point get to the edge of our understanding and need to acknowledge a certain amount of mystery.

If you can completely get your mind around God, you're probably not thinking about him at all but a man-made, scaled-down approximation. The trinity, the incarnation, the holiness of God, even the way the Bible has both human and divine authorship, are all far beyond fathoming out. That is not to say that we cannot know anything about God. He has revealed many things to us, not so that we can work it all out, but so that we can live it all out.

HOMING IN ON A HEALING MIRACLE

At the end of the day, it's hard to learn a language if you never open your mouth to speak it. This dynamic of theory and practice is especially true when it comes to exercising our God given authority, which is what our first healing miracle in Matthew chapters 8 and 9 is all about. In chapter 1 we took something of an overview. Now let's home in on an individual healing miracle:

> When he entered Capernaum, a centurion came forward to him, appealing to him, "Lord, my servant is lying paralyzed at home, suffering terribly." And he said to him, "I will come and heal him." But the centurion replied, "Lord, I am not worthy to have you come under my roof, but only say the word, and my servant will be healed. For I too am a man under authority, with soldiers under me. And I say to one, 'Go,' and he goes, and to another, 'Come,' and he comes, and to my servant, 'Do this,' and he does it." When Jesus heard this, he marvelled and said to those who followed him, "Truly, I tell you, with no one in Israel have I found

such faith. I tell you, many will come from east and west and recline at table with Abraham, Isaac, and Jacob in the kingdom of heaven, while the sons of the kingdom will be thrown into the outer darkness. In that place there will be weeping and gnashing of teeth." And to the centurion Jesus said, "Go; let it be done for you as you have believed." And the servant was healed at that very moment. (Matthew 8:5–13)

SICKNESS IS BAD

When you think about how difficult life must have been for a paralysed person in those days, it's not surprising that the centurion's servant was "suffering terribly". God created us with bodies that form an integral part of who we are and how we relate to the world around us. After our current bodies return to dust, the Bible says we will get a new, perfected body rising from the dead "seed" of the old. Losing most of our ability to move is incredibly debilitating. Even today, with all our technological and medical help, life for someone with severe paralysis must be incredibly hard. What, therefore, must it have been like for this man in the first century? The Greek word translated here as "suffering" literally means "torture", and I'm sure that that was exactly how it felt.

Our hearts go out to people in such terrible situations, and we want them to be well. Instinctively we think this is wrong and want to do all we can to help. And that's what the centurion was doing. He wanted his servant to be well. But what about God? Does he want people to be well too?

We can answer that by seeing what Jesus says, but first, I find what he doesn't say as telling as what he does. He doesn't say, "Sorry, he's being punished for something he has done wrong and needs to endure it as spiritual medicine, good for the soul." He never says anything remotely like that. Ever.

When responding to the question of why a man was born blind, Jesus says, "So that the works of God might be displayed in his life" (John 9:3). While God may well have been working in the man's life up to this point, the work of God in view here is surely the subsequent miraculous healing. After saying, "we must do the works of him who sent me" (John 9:4), Jesus heals him.

It's wonderfully true that we can glorify God in our lives by trusting him through difficult situations and circumstances, including long-term sickness, but this must never be used as a reason to lower our expectation for healing. Surely John 9:3 raises our expectation for healing rather than lowers it. The point of the passage is that God's kingdom advances, and God's glory is revealed as people are made well.

When the centurion tells Jesus about his sick servant, his immediate response is to go and heal him. He's like a good parent who rushes to help a child who has had a bad fall. "My servant is sick", says the centurion. "Ok, I'll go and heal him", says Jesus. Can you see how straightforward it is? Jesus is predisposed to do something about it. He doesn't need persuading. Consistent with every time he was faced with sickness and suffering, he was willing to heal. Sickness is never viewed by Jesus as anything other than bad, and he never dealt with it in any other way than to heal it. This surely must shape our response too. One would expect the followers of Jesus to be similarly compassionate to those who are ill and completely confident in Jesus' desire to heal them.

THE CENTURION'S AUTHORITY

I am struck by the centurion's bold but humble request. Someone once said to me, "God will forgive me. That's his job." It's the same kind of attitude and lack of respect that leads some to drop litter because, "It's someone's job to pick it up." The trouble is, however, when we demand our rights from God, we are treading on very thin ice and might just get what we deserve! We would be much better off making requests of him based on his kindness, love, and grace. We can do this with confidence because God is gracious and kind, but we should do so humbly recognising that grace cannot be forced only freely given.

This is exactly how the centurion approaches Jesus. He wants his servant to be well and so humbly asks Jesus to heal him. He had every confidence in Jesus because he recognised him as "a man under authority" (Matthew 8:9).

In our culture of me, my rights, ill-discipline, and independence, we can miss the force of what the centurion says here. The Romans ruled an empire for well over half a millennium with one of the most disciplined military organisations that has ever existed. This centurion would have been a hardened military man who had worked his way up through the ranks over many years of solid soldiering. He would have had up to hundred men directly under his command, plus extra responsibilities in the legion or cohort.

As a centurion, he would have carried a big, hard, wooden stick with which to beat disobedient or disrespectful soldiers. I read an account once of a centurion whose nickname translates as "Gimme-Another". He used to beat soldiers so hard with his stick that it broke, at which point he would call out, "Gimme-another", and continue dishing out punishment with a fresh rod. In extreme cases of disobedience or desertion, a soldier could even be executed. These things are pretty grim but knowing them helps us breathe the atmosphere in which this man lived.

If the centurion told a soldier to "Go", he would go. If he told him to "Come", he would come. There would be no pause or questioning. The soldier would not think about it; he would just do it. Failure to obey would result in swift and harsh punishment, witnessed by the whole unit.

But think about it. In front of the centurion are a large number of strong men who could easily overpower him. He's got one wooden stick, and they've got hundreds of sharp, shiny metal swords. Why do they go where he tells them to? Why do they instantly and unquestioningly obey him in everything? It's not because of his own power it's because he is a man under authority.

Caesar had authorised the centurion to lead these men, and if a soldier rebelled, the unimaginably huge power of the Roman Empire would crush him into the ground. What's more, Caesar's rule extended over such a wide area that they could never hope to run fast enough, for long enough, to get away. Even if the whole legion rebelled, they would be "decimated": a term referring to the execution of every tenth man in the unit.

Authority is backed up with power. Without authority, what you see is what you get, which in this case is a man in a skirt with a stick. With authority, however, you get the entire Roman Empire in your face and on your back until you do as you are told. You may not be able to see it, but step out of line and you will soon be made to feel it.

JESUS' AUTHORITY

This rough, battle hardened centurion recognised Jesus as a man *with* authority and, therefore, as someone *under* authority. He recognised, as others did, a kingdom force behind this ordinary looking man in sandals, and Mark's gospel helps us understand how. Right at the start of Jesus' ministry we are told that:

> The people were all so amazed that they asked each other, "What is this? A new teaching—and with authority! He even gives orders to evil spirits and they obey him." (Mark 1:27)

Jesus' teaching was fresh, opening the windows on the stale air of the religious leaders' doctrines, but it was the miracles, most of all, that demonstrated his authority. He "drove out evil spirits with a word" (Matthew 8:16–17), commanded a paralysed man and even a dead girl to get up (Matthew 9:1–8; Luke 8:54), and told a leper to "Be clean" (Matthew 8:1–5). Jesus told sick bodies what to do, and they did it. He told demons to leave, and they left.

Jesus said that he could do nothing on his own: "the Son can do nothing of his own accord, but only what he sees the Father doing" (John 5:19–20). He was chosen, anointed, qualified, and sent into the world to carry out a divine commission. The centurion saw in Jesus something that he recognised: a man under authority backed up by the immense power of an unstoppable empire.

OUR AUTHORITY

But it wasn't just Jesus who exercised this sort of authority; his disciples did too. At the end of these two action-packed chapters, which describe one healing after another, Matthew tells us that Jesus sent his twelve disciples out to do the same things that he had done:

> He called his twelve disciples to him and gave them authority to drive out evil spirits and to heal every disease and sickness. (Matthew 10:1)

What's more, he gave the same authority to the seventy-two unnamed disciples, who came back amazed, saying, "Lord, even the demons submit to us in your name" (Luke 10:17).

We often emphasise Jesus' uniqueness, and rightly so, but we can trip over it in an unhelpful way. You see, Jesus did not come to sort everything out so we could passively wait and watch. He came to establish a new pattern and template for humanity. Adam, the first man, was the first template. He was given authority to rule over the earth and fill it with God's glory. Tragically, he disobeyed God, rebelling against his loving authority and becoming weak and enslaved to other things. All subsequent people are cast from the same mangled mould and continue to follow in Adam's faulty footsteps. Jesus came as the last Adam to create a new template for all those who put their faith in him.

Jesus is uniquely sinless, but by God's grace, we have his righteousness credited to us and are becoming increasingly righteous in our thoughts and actions. Jesus is uniquely and eternally the only begotten Son of the Father, yet we are adopted as sons into our heavenly Father's family (Galatians 4:1–5; Ephesians 1:4–5). Jesus' suffering and death uniquely paid for the sin of the world, yet the Bible tells us that as we face hardship for the sake of his name, we share in his sufferings (Romans 8:17). Jesus is the firstborn from among the dead, which means that his was the first body to die perishable and be raised imperishable. In the same way, our body will be sown in weakness and raised in power (1 Corinthians 15:42).

We can go on: Jesus is uniquely seated in the heavenly realms at his Father's side, yet we are seated with him in these same heavenly places (Ephesians 2:6). Jesus was anointed by the Spirit to preach the good news and give sight to the blind, yet now we have received that same Spirit and that same anointing (Romans 8:9–11). He is the one who has been given all authority, uniquely as the Son, yet he has given us authority (Luke 10:19) so that by the Spirit, we might continue to assail the gates of hell and destroy the works of Satan.

Sometimes we read about Jesus doing the works of his Father in supernatural power and think that God has a different plan for us that looks nothing like the life that Jesus led. That is just not true. The two should look very similar. The same Spirit inspired speech, the same Spirit empowered healing and deliverance, and unfortunately, yes, the same Spirit saturated suffering, as we face hardship for Jesus' name. Basically, if Jesus isn't our role model and neither are his disciples, then who are we basing our lives on?

It's not just a few special people who get to do the things Jesus did. It's all who have put their faith in Jesus and are being transformed to be more like him. Do not be deceived, you have authority to destroy the kingdom of darkness and bring in the kingdom of God.

EXERCISING AUTHORITY

To get practical with this we need to understand the dynamics of authority a little better. Imagine you are a newly qualified teacher walking along a school corridor to take your first class. As you approach, you hear sounds of excited chatter, desk lids banging, and chairs being scraped across the floor. Your sweaty palm slips on the door knob as you turn it and step into the fray. Immediately, there is a flurry of activity as students fly to their seats. Amazingly, they straighten their backs, fold their hands neatly in front of them, and fix their eyes on you, ready to obey your every word.

To exercise authority, sometimes all you need to do is turn up. Just because you are recognised as a teacher, everyone will be quiet and get ready to learn. If they do, you can be sure that they are familiar with authority and the power that backs it up. They recognise you as someone in authority and act accordingly.

When the centurion turned up, every soldier would stand to attention, their eyes on him, ready to obey. If any of them had been doing something wrong, they would have stopped immediately. Sometimes people will get well as a church worships together or the Bible is taught without healing even being mentioned. I remember one lady whose arthritic finger suddenly got better while I was preaching on something totally unrelated to healing. As Jesus' name is lifted up, sickness sometimes just leaves. On another occasion, I was praying for a guy to be filled with the Spirit, and he was suddenly healed from chronic pain in his hand. Just turning up and being recognised is sometimes enough.

We need to ask ourselves if we are recognisable as a Christian or indistinguishable from those around us. We may be naturally visible with a fish on our car and worship music blaring out on the stereo, but what about spiritually discernible? Are we, like Jesus, baptised in water, filled with the Spirit, resisting temptation, and spending time with God in the secret place of private prayer? What's our spiritual hygiene like? What do you smell like in the Spirit? Is there a whiff of fear or a waft of faith about you? Is there a stink of gossip or a fragrance of prayer? It would probably be going too far to ask if you are wearing Holy Spirit aftershave or perfume, but I'm sure you get the point!

Students love to wind up teachers who don't know their authority or how to wield it. When you turn up, does the enemy smile and say: "Oh, here's that push over. We can get them to do whatever we want. They don't know who they really are. Christianity is just another thing they do. There's the button for anger, and there's the one for lust, and if he tries to get serious, there is always his unforgiveness and insecurity."

Let's get back to the classroom and your first teaching post. Imagine that on this occasion the class is a little less compliant. They don't notice you come in, or at least they pretend not to. Perhaps some sit down, but the noise level stays high. In that situation, you might have to speak up and say something. Hopefully a simple "Please sit down and stop talking" will be enough.

The centurion would have phrased commands a little more forcefully, but the principle is still the same. He said, "Come", and they would come, "Go", and they would go, "Do", and they did. Jesus also sorted things out with a well-chosen word or two. He even told a storm to "Be quiet!":

> He got up, rebuked the wind and said to the waves, "Quiet! Be still!" Then the wind died down and it was completely calm. (Mark 4:39)

Usually, we need to issue specific commands and state what we want to happen. "Body, be healed", or "Ears, be opened in Jesus' name." The fact that it's in Jesus' name is important as he is the authority we are acting under and the source of power that will back us up.

Now, it's nice when things go smoothly but sometimes they don't, and authority can be rebelliously and aggressively resisted. As a teacher, perhaps you get ignored. Or worse still a child turns round, looks you in the eye and says, "No! Make me." Another quips, "Who are you to tell me what to do?" and grins around at his classmates. So, who are you, and what are you going to do?

Well, the worst thing you can do is back down mumbling something along the lines of, "Oh, sorry, it's just that I wanted to get your attention to do a bit of teaching, but that's ok, I can see you're busy. Carry on and I'll come back later." In such situations we need to know who we are and the authority that we have. Authority is the right to exercise power, so when your authority is questioned, and you are made to feel small, stupid, and weak, you need to know you are in the right and that it is not you who is being resisted, but God. It will not, therefore, be your power backing up your words, but God's.

As a teacher you might need to continue exercising your authority by repeating the command to "Sit down!" but this time, with a bit more emphasis, knowing that obedience is non-negotiable.

If things should reach a complete impasse, you might ask others to come and stand with you. A teacher has the head teacher behind them and can call them in if necessary. Far from undermining your authority, that actually affirms it. You see, when a class is not recognising a teacher's authority, they are not recognising the authority of the head teacher who gave them that authority in the first place. The head teacher is in turn backed up by local government, then the national government, then the police, the army, and if things get really out of hand the SAS can be called in! Mercifully that's a rare occurrence, but the point is that a teacher in a class room is not isolated and alone because they are under authority. They have massive power backing them up, and so does every follower of Jesus.

Jesus' disciples were sent out in twos. We also, as the church, should act together as we advance the kingdom with our different strengths and insights. We need to encourage and support one another in ministry and prayer. If our authority is resisted, we can call in others to stand with us, or go back to God in prayer and fasting, calling out to him to back up his Son's name. Then we step out again in authority.

LEARNING THE LANGUAGE OF HEALING

Exercising authority is very practical. It's one thing to know you have it, but quite another to actually walk in it. A teacher's experience of exercising authority is likely to be very different at the end of their career than at the beginning. Over time, through trial and error, input and advice, and continual day in day out practice, they learn how to walk in the authority they have.

Stepping into a class room of unruly children for the first time takes guts, and so does exercising our spiritual authority over sickness and disease. As we do so though, we will learn to walk with greater confidence and see more bodies brought into line with God's coming kingdom. Who knows how many more people will be healed as we pluck up the courage to command bodies to be well? Let's be confident in our God given authority that we have both the permission and power to heal. I really want to learn New Testament Greek, but I am even more determined to become fluent in God's wonderful language of healing.

QUESTIONS

1) Do you have a skill that required a lot of practice to develop? How long did it take you to get really good at it? What kept you going? What will motivate you to keep praying for people to be healed?

2) Are there any burning questions that you have about healing that you have not been able to find good answers to? Have they hindered you from believing God for healing? How can you prevent that from happening in the future?

3) Are you in any positions of authority? How have you learned to exercise that authority in practice? What do you do when it is resisted? How will an understanding of this dynamic help you as you step out in authority to heal the sick?

3. THE COST OF HEALING

"He took our illnesses and bore our diseases."
Matthew 8:17

LIVING IN THE GAP

We have been focusing on chapters 8 and 9 of Matthew's gospel where Jesus healed one person after another. He did this out of compassion, demonstrating who he was and backing up what he said. We have seen how he sent his disciples out to do the same: proclaiming the good news of the kingdom and demonstrating its powerful advance through supernatural healing.

In pressing forward, believing wholeheartedly that God wants to heal the sick, we are stepping into the gap between our current experience and a biblically based expectation. By doing so, we are entering a fierce battleground where the kingdom of heaven is being extended through faith, and like any battleground, it is not an easy place to be. There is blood, sweat, and tears; victories and defeats; advances and setbacks.

I have heard reports recently of God healing a damaged wrist, a knee, and two painful and debilitating back problems as people in our church prayed for others in the name of Jesus. We may not have seen the dead being raised just yet, but we have seen some genuine improvement in a few conditions and are really grateful to God. However, I know that a lot of people, myself included, have not yet received much needed and sought after healing.

Even in situations where many are healed, I am acutely aware of those who remain sick. While I don't want to focus on what God is not doing, I do want to be aware of where his kingdom still needs advancing. I also do not want to leave people who are already suffering even more vulnerable to the enemy's lies and attacks. I know there are many who have left healing meetings rejoicing in the healing of others, encouraged in their faith for healing, but processing the reality that they themselves are still not well. Others stand with those who daily face the pain and discomfort of sickness while trusting that God is willing and able to heal.

The question, therefore, arises as to how you persevere faithfully in the gap—when it's not an issue of putting together a tidy theology but living with a broken body. You are hearing and receiving God's word, but your faith is under daily attack from discomfort and disappointment.

Answering this question is not straightforward because Jesus healed everybody he came across, and the disciples seemed to have a great deal of success too. On one occasion when the disciples didn't see instant healing, Jesus points to their faith, their prayer life, and possibly fasting, as keys (Mark 9:19–29). That is helpful, and we should keep pressing into God in these ways, but it's not the whole story. Sometimes things just don't turn out as we had hoped and prayed for even though we thought we had real faith for healing.

In the book of Acts and the New Testament letters there are clear indicators that not everyone was in perfect health all the time. Although Paul saw amazing miracles happen, both Paul himself, (Galatians 4:13) and others around him experienced periods of sickness. Paul left his friend Trophimus sick in Miletus (2 Timothy 4:20). His helper Timothy struggled with frequent health problems, (1 Timothy 5:23) and Epaphroditus was so ill he "almost died" (Philippians 2:27). The unapologetic, matter-of-fact way in which these illnesses are mentioned, indicates that it was not totally unheard of for people to get ill, even with the apostles around. However, while it can be a help knowing that even Paul must have prayed at times and not seen immediate results, we should avoid interpreting these things in a way that lowers our expectation for healing. We need to keep in mind that Jesus healed everyone who came to him and that the early church, however inspirational and foundational, was a starting point and a work in progress.

A CLEAR VIEW OF THE CROSS

So what do we do when we don't have all the answers, when life is messy and confusing? Well, I used to go for walks on the South Downs to relax and gather my thoughts. That was helpful, but a walk on the hills can only have a superficial effect. There is, however, a hill we can go to that orientates us in the fog of disappointment and renews our joy and strength. It's called Calvary, and it's the place where Jesus bled and died for us. When wrestling with these difficult questions it's best to take the shortest route to the cross, and in Matthew's account of the healing miracles of Jesus we get a signpost to one of the best views of the cross in the whole Bible. If we are to continue to reach for fruit in supernatural healing, we need to stop and take a long look.

Matthew quotes a line from Isaiah 53 and sees in this prophecy the background and context for Jesus' healing ministry. It's as if we have been whisked up, along with the prophet, to some high vantage point where we get a crystal clear view of the cross, hundreds of years before Jesus was even born:

And when Jesus entered Peter's house, he saw his

mother-in-law lying sick with a fever. He touched her hand, and the fever left her, and she rose and began to serve him. That evening they brought to him many who were oppressed by demons, and he cast out the spirits with a word and healed all who were sick. This was to fulfil what was spoken by the prophet Isaiah: "He took our illnesses and bore our diseases." (Matthew 8:14–17)

Isaiah wrote what is arguably the pinnacle of Old Testament Messianic prophecy—the clearest image, through the longest time telescope, of the most significant moment in history. When NASA scientists want to accelerate a space craft without expending fuel, they perform a manoeuvre called a "slingshot". They fly the space craft close to a planet and let the gravitational pull increase its speed. The interstellar craft hurtles towards the planet and is briefly pulled around it in a partial orbit before being catapulted back out into space at incredible speed. The cross is the spiritual mass around which God's purpose in creation slingshots around.

Let's look at this majestic passage and draw out some truths that will speed us on our way as we reach for supernatural healing. Why not spend a few moments now reading Isaiah 53:1–12 and taking in the view?

BELIEVE IT OR NOT

First, Isaiah sees a message that is going to be proclaimed and the critical question, the most important aspect of this message, is "Who will believe [it]?" (Isaiah 53:1a). God has always been looking for faith—for people to believe him and trust what he says. The sad implication here is that many people won't. The message will be so unexpected, so amazing, so shocking in its content that many will ignore it, or dismiss it out of hand. Some will even take it upon themselves to oppose it.

It's not that there won't be lots of evidence to back it up. There will be. It's not that there won't be reasonable arguments to support it. There will be. It's just that people's hearts will be so hardened against this message that it will take an act of supernatural revelation for it to be accepted.

The content of the message is about the "arm of the Lord" (Isaiah 53:1b) which is an Old Testament metaphor for God's power and strength. Matthew states that the message is about Jesus, and it doesn't take much imagination to see him here. God's power, therefore, will be supremely demonstrated in the person of his Son. So the key question to be asked becomes: "Who has believed in Jesus?"

Next, we might ask "Who is this message from?", and who is the "our" and the "us" referring to in Isaiah 53 verses 1 and 2? Many possibilities present themselves. It could be the prophets, or Israel, or the nations, but I don't think we need to pin it down too firmly. To me, it reads as a group of people who had once rejected this message and nearly missed it but now, having embraced it, have become messengers themselves. It seems to me that Isaiah is seeing those who have believed and are now declaring the message to the nations. Maybe it was the first disciples who "reported" what they saw. It would certainly apply to Christians now, for when you believe this message it becomes your message, and you join the next wave of messengers to the world.

JESUS' SUFFERING

While verse 1 talked about the message, verse 2 starts with "He" and tells us more about a person. Like the message, he is not at first sight very attractive. It's not really referring to his looks; rather, that he didn't have the money, fame, and glamour that tend to catch our eye.

Jesus was nothing like your favourite pop idol or movie star. He was born into a poor family in a little village in the Middle East. He didn't live in a big house or wear fancy clothes, and like most men, he learnt a trade and worked hard to earn a living. For much of his life you could have walked past him on the street without noticing anything out of the ordinary. You might have paid him for a job, engaged in some small talk, and then got on with your day.

While he did have some sort of popularity for a short time, in the end his enemies got their way, and he was sentenced to death by crucifixion.

At his trial Jesus hardly said a word, and for much of it he remained completely silent. He went through it without protesting his innocence, pleading for mercy, or resisting in any way. As I read the accounts I wonder, "Why doesn't he say something?" Isaiah's vivid description of a lamb, silent as it is led to the slaughter, captures the scene perfectly (Isaiah 53:7).

During and after the trial, Jesus was beaten, bullied, and humiliated by the Roman guards. After that, as was the custom, he was brutally whipped with a flagrum. The metal attached at various intervals along its leather straps would have made short work of his skin, ripping into the flesh beneath. The Romans had become incredibly skilful at inflicting the maximum amount of pain during the flogging while keeping their victim alive for what was to come next. This was just the warm-up.

Isaiah sees a man so disfigured he is virtually unrecognisable (Isaiah 52:14): a bleeding mess of tissue and bone from which men turned away and hid their faces (Isaiah 53:3). If I had been there and witnessed it, rather than having merely read about it or watched films depicting it, I'm sure it would have left me deeply traumatised. It was truly appalling. After the beating and scourging, Jesus' flesh would be hanging off him in ribbons. Isaiah speaks of the "suffering of his soul", (Isaiah 53:11) which sounds like a very deep kind of suffering indeed, and hints that something far more than mere physical affliction is going on here. Jesus experienced some of the worst pain and torment that anyone has ever had to endure: emotionally, physically, and spiritually. It's certainly fair to say that he was a man intimately acquainted with grief and sorrow (Isaiah 53:3).

Next, Isaiah saw a man who was "pierced", "run through", "skewered", or "slain" (Isaiah 53:5). Once again he is spot on. Crucifixion meant being nailed to a cross with long iron nails, and in Jesus' case, a spear was also thrust into his side to make sure he was dead (John 19:34).

Make no mistake about it, crucifixion was a form of execution designed to cause the maximum pain over the longest period of time. What's more, to quite literally add insult to injury, those that could stomach the sight mocked Jesus mercilessly. It's even possible that some people were crucified at eye level to facilitate this kind of scornful derision. "Who does he think he is?" they said. "The King of the Jews? What kind of saviour gets himself nailed to a cross? What a joke! He can't even save himself."

Then, after hours of agony, Jesus finally died. When a spear was stuck into his side, a mixture of blood and water flowed out, testifying to the severe trauma he had suffered. Satisfied that he was dead, the soldiers then took his body down from the cross.

Isaiah sees Jesus being with wicked men in his death but also mentions a rich man. From the gospel account, we now know that Jesus was crucified along with two criminals and that a rich man put Jesus' corpse in the grave intended for his own body (Isaiah 53:8–9).

One thing we can say from all this is that God knows what it's like to suffer and to endure the most excruciating agony. He knows what it's like to be pinned down and paralysed. In times of sickness, we can draw strength from knowing that God knows what we are experiencing because he has gone through it himself. We may not understand why we continue to suffer, but having the abiding presence of a God who himself has endured so much, is a real help. As we follow Jesus in healing the sick, we need not lose sight of him in our own suffering.

He has gone ahead of us in that too and can be incredibly close at such times.

OUR GUILT AND SIN

The man that Isaiah saw suffered terribly (Isaiah 53:4). But why? Was God punishing him for having done something wrong? No, Isaiah says he was innocent (Isaiah 53:9). It turns out he was punished for what *we* had done wrong: for *our* "transgressions" and *our* "iniquities" (Isaiah 53:5).

It's interesting how words go out of fashion. When was the last time you referred to something good as "spiffing" or heard a scatterbrain called a "flibbertigibbet"? These days calling an attractive person "toothsome" could be misunderstood! Similarly, the words "transgressions" and "iniquities" have fallen from common use. I guess we think "out of sight, out of mind", but a forgotten rose is still a rose and its thorns more likely to prick.

As I reach for other words that mean something similar, many sound equally quaint and old-fashioned. "Sin" is the nearest, but we could equally add "depravity", "perversity", "guilt", "rebellion", "missing the mark", "doing evil", or "not doing the good that we should". These aren't the sorts of words and phrases that we comfortably apply to ourselves, but they describe us at one time or another, nonetheless.

Forget the terms for a moment. We've all done things wrong: things that we are not proud of; things we are ashamed of even. Most of us would admit that at one time or another we have lied, cheated, been unfaithful (with our thoughts if not our actions), been self-centred, thought unkindly about others, gossiped, misused sexual intimacy outside of marriage, or simply not helped where we might have, in the way we could have, with the attitude we should have had.

Isaiah sees the whole human race, all of us, as being like a flock of silly sheep. We have all wandered away from God, gone our own way, and done our own thing (Isaiah 53:6). We have foolishly followed others, wandering around in circles and into danger. Instead of loving God and putting him first, we gave other things the prime place in our lives and followed work, food, fame, or fortune.

The plain fact is it's *not* ok to do these things. Did we think it would be? Did we think that there would be no real and lasting consequences? Can morality really just be a personal preference, a cultural illusion, or a psychological side effect? Some think it's a purely evolutionary phenomenon and reduce morality into biology. Others think "right" and "wrong" are simply quaint and outdated religious fabrications.

But God doesn't disappear when we stop thinking about him, and we don't stop sinning when we stop using the word or change its meaning. There is a Holy God in heaven who is so pure and good that he will not let evil go unpunished. On the cross he demonstrates his anger and wrath against sin. You can be sure that God is just, and that not only will every evil act done against you be punished, but all the wrong things we have done will be punished in full too.

I used to think "I'm not that bad." Maybe I deserved a slap on the wrist for being a "naughty boy" and to be given the chance to do better. Isaiah sees it differently however, and so does God. The cross challenges, condemns, and recalibrates our moral assessment of ourselves because while we were brazenly grazing on toxic grass, one unpopular sheep was silently being led away to be slaughtered on our behalf.

THE FORGIVENESS OF GOD

Isaiah 53 is primarily about Jesus being punished in our place for our sin. Even when it uses the word "infirmities" it does so in a mainly metaphorical sense, referring to our "sin sickness". The context and its use in the New Testament tell us this passage is mainly about freedom from the guilt and punishment of sin. The word "healed", as used in this context, means first and foremost sorting out our sin problem, our moral failing and standing before God. Peter, another of Jesus' disciples writes:

> He himself bore our sins in his body on the tree, that we might die to sin and live to righteousness. (1 Peter 2:24)

He then quotes from Isaiah to make his point: "with his wounds we are healed" (Isaiah 53:5). He is talking about righteousness, that is, right living and right standing before God. He is talking about wandering sheep returning to the true shepherd. It certainly doesn't seem like Peter has physical healing at the forefront of his mind.

As much as we press forward believing God for supernatural healing, we must not lose sight of the central truth that our sin is forgiven. Our true source of joy is that our sins are forgiven, and we can know God's presence and his love. Let hardship and suffering and sickness do their worst, they cannot remove or change the fact that my name is "written in the Lamb's book of life" (Revelation 21:27). Though my body may be dying and will one day return to dust, it is well with my soul. One day, God will recreate from the dead and dusty seed of my old body, a new, eternal, and glorious one (1 Corinthians 15:50–58).

Let's get things into perspective. Sin is by far our biggest problem not physical sickness. Please hear me: we need to engage in an all-out war on sickness because God wants people to be well even more than we do, and healing is part of the vocabulary in which he wants to speak to a sick world. However, if we die without being reconciled to God both our bodies and our souls will perish forever—separated from the source of life and love. Jesus points out that it's one thing for the body to perish but quite another for the soul to be destroyed (Matthew 10:28). He talks about a place of weeping and torment, a place of soul squirming sorrow and ongoing agony and death (Matthew 25:30; Mark 9:48). Alternatively, because of Jesus' death and resurrection, we can know God's love for all eternity. We can live with him forever in a new heaven and a new earth, free from pain and suffering and sickness and death (Revelation 21:4).

THE LOVE OF GOD

Have you seen those make-up adverts with the slogan, "Because you're worth it"? They play on our need to be valued and loved. Deep down, though, we all know that no matter how many times a multinational cosmetic company says, "you're worth it", the feeling wipes off with the make-up, and it is plain old us again. The truth is we won't know true love, value, or worth until we recognise what Jesus did for us on the cross. On the cross Jesus counted out our worth, not in loose change or even gold bars, but in pints of his own blood; one, two, three, four ... until he was completely spent.

Jesus went to the cross to pay for the things we did. We deserve to be punished and crushed for what we have done, but Jesus loves us so much that he was prepared to be punished and crushed in our place. Have you ever had anyone else do something like that for you? Maybe you think love is about getting. Maybe the people who said they loved you were just taking from you. Well, Jesus is different; he gave himself up for you.

Jesus suffered in our place because he really, really wanted to. He loves us that much. On the cross he saw us individually and together as the church, his beautiful bride, and he counted us well worth the cost:

> Out of the anguish of his soul he shall see and be satisfied. (Isaiah 53:11)

The New Testament puts it like this:

> For God so loved the world, that he gave his only Son,
> that whoever believes in him should not perish but
> have eternal life. (John 3:16)

Jesus so loved us, so loved you, and so loved me that he was prepared to stand in our place and take the punishment that we deserve. Each time the whip tore into his body, each time a nail was hammered deeper in to his wrists, each time he pushed himself up to take a breath of air, he was loving us by bearing the cost of our sin, loving us by paying the price of our rebellion.

While it's certainly true that Jesus loved us, John 3:16 is specifically talking about God the Father's love for us. I'm a father, and there are times when I think I feel my children's pain more deeply than they do. I can't even begin to imagine what it cost the Father to give us his Son. What amazing love!

In the gospel, there is a worth that can be found by declaring our bankruptcy, a dignity that can be gained by admitting our shame, and a love that can be known by recognising our unloveliness. John, after a lifetime of knowing Jesus, wrote this:

> This is love, not that we loved God but that he loved us
> and sent his Son to be the propitiation for our sins.
> (1 John 4:10)

"Propitiation" is another old-fashioned word meaning to "turn away wrath", and we need to understand this concept in order to know God's love for us. God was angry with us because of our sin. Yet because of his great love, he gave up his Son so that we might be brought into his family and adopted as sons and daughters.

Therefore, as we reach for fruit in supernatural healing, God's love for us in Christ must remain our place of security, joy, rest, and confidence. It's only because of the cross that we know God's love for us.

If someone else gets healed and you don't, does it mean that God doesn't love you as much? No. Why? *Because of the cross.* If God uses someone else to bring supernatural healing, does that mean he loves them more than you? That they are more worthy of being used by him? No. Why? *Because of the cross.*

We need not look to our present situation or comfort or ability or wealth or health or gifts to determine God's love for us. We look to the cross, and the answer is always the same: "I loved *you* so much that I sent my son to die for *you.*" It's like infinity in mathematics—a number by definition such that there is no greater number. Infinity plus one (or minus one for that matter) is still infinity. In the same way, there is no love greater than the infinite love displayed on the cross. There is no "cross plus one" love.

Why do I say all this? Simply because we need to reach for healing not as needy orphans, but as dearly loved sons and daughters. We do not come cup in hand to God, begging for scraps, hoping he is in a good mood today. Rather, we have been welcomed into his throne room to enjoy the riches of his grace to us in Christ. Our destiny is to take part in his plan to establish his glorious kingdom on earth.

THE SOVEREIGNTY OF GOD

One of the unusual things about this passage in Isaiah is that though the suffering servant dies, he is still around to "see his offspring". He will "be satisfied", "justify many", have a "portion among the great", and "divide the spoils". It looks like he will be quite busy for a dead person! This riddle is solved by the resurrection. Jesus would die, but God would "prolong his days" by raising him from the dead. His "offspring" (Isaiah 53:10) are those who believe this message and are born again by the Spirit into the family of God.

At this point, it's good to remind ourselves that we are reading prophecy. God spoke this out before it happened. Not only did Jesus rise from the dead, but God said he would do so hundreds of years beforehand. God was not surprised when Jesus was arrested, tried, and crucified. In fact, he had determined in advance that all these things would happen (Acts 2:23). What looked like a total disaster on the ground was actually the decisive step in achieving heaven's purposes. At just the moment when it looked like all was lost, all was won. Everything was running exactly according to plan.

That does not mean that God betrayed his Son; Judas did that. Neither did God falsely accuse Jesus; the Jewish leaders of the time did that. And, of course, Jesus' Father did not nail Jesus to the cross; it was the Roman soldiers who hammered in the nails. But as these evil things were being done, God was working through it all to bring about a supreme good. God's best came through men's worst.

The cross, therefore, should change my perspective on every bad situation I see. Not only does it tell me that God hates sin and evil and will come against them with the full force of his wrath, it also tells me that God can and does, work through them for a greater good. Yes, even through sickness and ill health. Satan intends these things for evil, but God super-intends them for good (Genesis 15:20). The detail and timing of how he works that out are often hidden from us. Sometimes we can look back and see the good that God brought out of a time of suffering, but most of the time, frankly, we can't. At such times the cross gives us confidence to keep trusting. The few hours that Jesus hung on the cross must have seemed like an eternity, but three days later everything looked very different.

The cross reassures me that everything will work for the good of those who love God (Romans 8:28), that his purposes are unstoppable, that we can trust him, and that he will not hold back on us (Romans 8:32). Knowing these things helps us navigate our way through mysteries we don't understand. It's because of the cross that we can worship Jesus and enjoy the love of God in all circumstances, including hardship and ill health. It's because of the cross that we know all sickness and death will one day be gone forever. And it's because of the cross that we are encouraged to ask God for physical healing, and even resurrection, in the here and now.

HEALING ACCOMPLISHED ON THE CROSS

It is important to grasp all of these truths and hold them together because we are not just weeping spectators of evil but soldiers commissioned to fight on the frontline against it. We may not know everything, but we do know this: we have a part to play in how God brings glorious good out of Satan's horrible sicknesses. One way we should seek to do that is by reaching out for supernatural healing in the lives of those around us. Just like Jesus did, and just like his disciples did.

While the primary thought in Isaiah 53 is sin bearing, Matthew does not let us leave it there. The Hebrew words in Isaiah 53:4, often translated as "griefs" and "sorrows", can also mean physical sicknesses and diseases:

> This was to fulfil what was spoken by the prophet Isaiah: "He took our illnesses and bore our diseases." (Matthew 8:17)

Matthew is saying that what Jesus was doing when he healed all those people was fulfilling a particular aspect of this rich prophetic passage in Isaiah. It may not be the primary meaning of Isaiah, but physical healing is included there all the same. Matthew is saying that when Jesus bore our spiritual sin problem on his shoulders, he was also taking the strain of our physical sickness problems too. Sin bearing and sickness bearing happened together. If we go back to the fall in the Garden of Eden we see that there is a link between sin and death, so Jesus is not doing two unrelated things here. The fact is that he paid for both. It cost him massively, and he did it out of love.

The Jesus who is concerned about our forgiveness is also concerned about our health. The Jesus who lifted the burden of our sin also wants to lift the pain of our sickness from us. Using a term that is currently in vogue, his work on the cross was "holistic". That said, I do not think Matthew is implying that accessing healing and accessing salvation work out the same in every detail. We need to be cautious before boldly proclaiming that healing is available on demand to all with enough faith.

So what is he saying? Well, first, that healing is an inseparable aspect of Jesus' ministry as prophesied by Isaiah, that our healing came at a great personal cost to Jesus, and that he did it because he loves us. Matthew is saying that there is not another transaction that occurred at some other time to secure our health.

Secondly, he is saying that the healing secured for us on the cross is not simply stored up for us in glorified resurrection bodies when Jesus comes back. Rather, it is an inseparable aspect of who Jesus is and how his kingdom is breaking out now. The healing power of the cross was breaking out through Jesus even before he was crucified, and it is certainly not turned off now that he has been raised from the dead. While I do have questions about exactly how much is available to us now, I am willing to put them on hold until I have at least surpassed the experience of the early church in this matter.

A FIRM FOUNDATION
The fact that this passage sits in the middle of our journey through Matthew 8 and 9 is so helpful. It reminds us of the centrality of the cross in all our thinking and actions. It provides insight into where our healing comes from and a context from which to reach out for it. The cross is the "horse" that goes in front of the "cart" of healing, and we should never

swap the two around in our thinking. If God "did not spare his own Son, but gave him up for us all, how will he not also with him graciously give us all things?" (Romans 8:32).

When you are building something tall like a skyscraper, the foundations are really important. In the same way, we need to reach out for supernatural healing from a firm base. Isaiah 53 provides this foundation for us in God's suffering, forgiveness, love, and sovereignty.

It also provides us with a good safety net. If God doesn't heal when we expect him to, we have no reason to question his love or his power. The cross trumps any argument we could construct against these things. He gave us his Son, so his love for us is proved beyond question. He worked through the evil schemes of Satan to bring about his good purposes, so his sovereignty is established.

The cross gives us confidence to say, "God will heal, but even if he doesn't heal right now, I will still trust him." Daniel and his friends had that kind of faith even before the cross, (Daniel 3:18) so we can certainly have it now. This robust kind of faith allows us to reach out for supernatural healing knowing that the bottom will not fall out of our world if things don't go as we expect. We are standing on the firm ground of the death and resurrection of Jesus and are being held in the sovereign hands of the God who works all things for our good.

In the security of God's love for us in Christ, therefore, let's believe for, and expect, more miraculous healing. Knowing that healing is a part of Jesus' work for us and has begun to be dispensed now with his message of forgiveness, we can do what he told his disciples to do; namely, preach the gospel and heal the sick. The gospel of forgiveness is central, but healing is an inseparable part of Jesus' work on the cross and of our proclamation of it.

QUESTIONS

1) Have you ever thought or felt that God does not love you? Why was that? How did you process those feelings?

2) How does the cross convince you of God's love for you?

3) How can you keep the cross central in your understanding of God, the world, and his purposes in it?

4) How does your understanding of all that was achieved for you on the cross help you reach out for fruit in supernatural healing?

4. THE HALLMARK OF HEALING

"that you may know that the
Son of Man has authority on
earth to forgive sins"
Matthew 9:6

THE STAMP OF AUTHENTICITY

I have a gold ring on my finger. At least it looks gold, but how can I tell if it really is gold? Well, if I take it off there are some little marks inside it. One of these marks is the date of my wedding. The other is what's called a hallmark, and its presence indicates that the item is made from genuine gold. Now, a hallmark can be forged, and gold is still gold even if it's not marked as such, but for almost seven hundred years this sort of imprint has been a key indicator of the genuine article. In this chapter we are going to look at a key hallmark of the gospel.

So far, in looking at a couple of chapters of Matthew's gospel, we have made the very basic but highly significant observation that Jesus really loves to heal people. We have read one account after another of him healing sick people and picked up on the fact that healing seems to be one of Jesus' favourite things to do.

This means that time spent studying what the Bible says about healing is not blowing something up out of all proportion or picking up some passing fad. There are so many ways we can be dissuaded or distracted from pursuing God for healing. It is vital, therefore, that we see what a big deal healing was in the life of Jesus. In pursuing healing we are not only responding to God's prophetic direction for the church today, but we are tapping into a wide and rich theme in both God's written word (the Bible) and his incarnate word (Jesus Christ).

In the last chapter we saw how Matthew linked the healing work of Jesus to his work on the cross. Most are agreed that it cost Jesus something to heal people. The controversy around healing, certainly among Bible believing Christians, is therefore not so much about where healing was purchased but about how much of it we can expect to enjoy now.

While that question may not be answered in as much detail as we would like, as we read the pages of the Bible an expectation builds to see a lot more people healed than we currently are. It may not be all healed instantly, right now, but it is certainly is a lot more healed, a lot quicker. Surely we can expect more people to be healed of cancer, arthritis, stomach problems, deafness, and blindness. We may have all sorts of questions, but we must not let them distract us from our commission.

In chapter 2 we looked at exercising our authority to heal and how we need to step out more and do it. The fact is that God has chosen to act primarily through you and me, the church, to see his "kingdom come on earth as it is in heaven" (Matthew 6:10).

So with these things in mind let's read our next passage:

> And getting into a boat he crossed over and came to his own city. And behold, some people brought to him a paralytic, lying on a bed. And when Jesus saw their faith, he said to the paralytic, "Take heart, my son; your

sins are forgiven." And behold, some of the scribes said to themselves, "This man is blaspheming." But Jesus, knowing their thoughts, said, "Why do you think evil in your hearts? For which is easier, to say, 'Your sins are forgiven,' or to say, 'Rise and walk'? But that you may know that the Son of Man has authority on earth to forgive sins"—he then said to the paralytic—"Rise, pick up your bed and go home." And he rose and went home. When the crowds saw it, they were afraid, and they glorified God, who had given such authority to men. (Matthew 9:1–8)

JESUS BRINGS HOPE

In verse 2 we are introduced to a paralysed man, who must have relied almost totally on his friends to wash, dress, eat, and go to the toilet. In all likelihood his muscles were emaciated and his skin covered in bed-sores. He had been afflicted like this for years, and there was no conceivable way things were ever going to change.

Then, on hearing that Jesus was coming to town, he and his friends experienced something that they had not experienced in a very long time: hope. No matter how bad things look, Jesus brings hope into every situation.

Either at the paralysed man's request or on their own initiative, his friends did the best thing that anyone could do: they brought him to Jesus. Although this story is about healing, and we don't want to lose sight of that, like every healing it's also a wonderful picture of salvation.

Each of us is spiritually paralysed and would not, on our own, seek out Jesus. When friends and those that care about us share the gospel with us, they bring us to him. People move house, give away their money, risk their reputation and their lives, all because they care about people so much that they want them to meet Jesus. Often we don't have the answers, but we can introduce people to the One who does.

FAITH FLARES

When Jesus looked at the faces peering through the gaping hole in the roof, he saw something that makes all the difference if human need is to be met by God's provision: faith. These men trusted that Jesus could help them, and Jesus saw it. Faith is so important to Jesus that he says:

> When the Son of Man comes, will he find faith on earth? (Luke 18:8)

Have you ever flown at night and looked out of the window? If you are flying over land all you see is pinpricks of light—not trees, not houses, not rivers, just light sources from windows, street lights, and cars. I remember landing in Boston late one evening and marvelling at the sparkling sea of lights spread out below me.

God sees faith a bit like that. Where there is faith it stands out like bright points of light; where there is none, it's just black. What does he see when he looks at you and me? When he casts his eye over our families, churches, cities, and nation? Is your heart and home visible to Jesus when he looks for faith? Would it be lit up, or dim and dark? Do you trust Jesus to help? Can he do it? Will he do it? If you have faith it's not invisible to Jesus but shines out brightly. In fact, he can see it now—a tiny twinkling light catching his eye.

Now, of course, God can do something without any apparent faith, and yes there may be times when we seem to have all the faith in the world, and yet we still don't see all that we had hoped for. At such times, we have to trust Jesus all the more in our limited knowledge and understanding. But we must never let these things overshadow or nullify the overwhelming emphasis in the Bible that God delights to exert his strength through faith in Jesus. Even now as you trust him in the darkness of your current situation, a faith flare is launched from your heart, catching his eye and grabbing his attention.

Let's take a moment to fly over chapters 8 and 9 of Matthew's gospel and see how much faith there is around. When a centurion asked Jesus to "just say the word", Jesus was astonished at his "great *faith*" and said, "Go; let it be done for you as you have *believed*" (Matthew 8:5–10, 13). When a woman said to herself, "if I only touch his cloak, I will be healed", Jesus turned to her and said, "Take heart, daughter, your *faith* has healed you" (Matthew 9:20–22). When Jesus asks some blind men if he is able to heal them, they respond "Yes, Lord." Touching their eyes Jesus said, "According to your *faith* will it be done to you" (Matthew 9:27–34).

There is no getting away from the primacy of faith in seeing God's kingdom come in healing power. God is looking for people who will trust him, even in the "smarter than thou" scientific West where belief in the supernatural is often seen as super-stupid. Believing that Jesus is willing and able to heal is essential if we are to reach for fruit in supernatural healing. Without that conviction we will give up far too easily, which would be a great shame as God wants to exert his power through our words and actions.

THE SECRET OF HAPPINESS

Jesus looks at the man lying on his mat in this appalling condition and says to him, "Take heart son." Can you hear the tenderness and concern of his address? It's so relational: "Take heart child." It means: "Don't be afraid, be encouraged! It's going to be ok. Help is at hand. You're going to be really happy about this." Jesus cares about this man and out of deep compassion he's going to meet his greatest need.

At this point in the account we might be thinking "Here we go, he's going to heal this man", but Jesus says something that comes as a surprise to us and probably to most people there at the time. He says, "Your sins are forgiven." You have got to admit that's a bit unexpected isn't it? Jesus sees a man who is so ill he can barely move and says, "Your sins are forgiven."

When I read this I thought, "Have I missed something here?", and the answer was "Yes, I have." If we think, "Oh, that's a shame" when Jesus says these words, then we have missed something massive. Imagine you walk up to someone in the street and ask them for directions. No sooner have you got the words out of your mouth than they push you away from them. You are about to shout something rather ungrateful, when a ten tonne truck rumbles past over the spot where moments ago you had been holding out your map. As the dust clears, revealing a crumpled body lying in the road, it dawns on you that you are alive because your saviour addressed your most pressing need.

Our biggest, most urgent problem is our sin, which will wreck our lives both now and beyond the grave for all eternity. Many ignore feelings of guilt, shame, and the fear of death, but I'm not so sure that the man on the mat had. For Jesus' statement to make any sense to him, he must have known he had a sin problem. He must have known that he had done things that were wrong and that those things not only damaged those around him, but separated him from God. Maybe lying on the mat for all those years gave him a better view of the oncoming traffic. He certainly would have had a lot of time to think about these things during the long days and longer nights as he lay there. Perhaps he had less pleasurable distractions than we do. He must have wished he could undo some of the things he had done and said. Perhaps he was aware that he didn't have long to live.

I'm speculating a bit, I know, so let's think about you and me. Are we more aware of what's on TV tonight than our moral failure before a Holy God? More concerned about burning the toast than failing to live up to God's perfect standard? Even if we are seriously ill, our greatest need is still to be forgiven and accepted by God.

So Jesus did not say "Take heart son, your sickness is healed", but "Your sins are forgiven." He looks at this man and sees his deepest, most immediate need is to have his sins forgiven. This is why Jesus came: to die on the cross, bearing our sin and shame (Mark 10:45; 1 Peter 2:34). If this problem is not sorted, not only will our body die but our soul will decay too. Everything that is good will recede forever from our experience.

Are you aware of the seriousness of your condition without God's forgiveness? You might be able to run a marathon but if you have done anything wrong in your life then you are essentially in the same position as this man.

How happy would you be (or were you) to hear Jesus say "Take heart, your sins are forgiven"? Would it mean the world to you? This is the source of our worship, our rejoicing, and our deepest happiness. Of course, we rejoice in other things. The birth of a baby, getting a job and being told your cancer is in remission are all cause for great celebration, but these are very secondary things compared to being forgiven by God. Spurgeon, the 19th century "prince of preachers", puts it well when he says:

> He bade him be comforted because his sins were forgiven—as if that would be a sufficient reason for rejoicing even if he should remain palsied! If he should be carried away from the presence of Christ upon his bed just as helpless as when he was let down from the roof into the middle of the crowded room, that would be quite a secondary matter compared with the all-important fact that his sins had been forgiven. (Spurgeon's Sermons: Volume 56, Number 3227, 1910)

If you are not happy, don't look for happiness in fame, riches, job, accomplishments or even health. A healthy body will not help you run away from your sin. No amount of good will ever undo the wrong you have done. God cannot be bribed and your fan club's praise won't impress him either. Of course, we want ourselves and others to be well, in good relationships, and engaged in meaningful labour, but these are not sources of true and everlasting happiness. They are but pleasant puddles to splash in compared to the deep ocean of joy that is knowing God's love and our sin forgiven.

THE PROOF IS IN THE PUDDING

Some of the people hearing Jesus' words at the time didn't see it that way though. To them, Jesus' pronouncement was not only flippant, but deeply blasphemous. How dare he take it upon himself to say, so lightly, "Your sins are forgiven." Doesn't he know how big a deal that is? If you sin against me then I can forgive you, but if you sin against someone else then my pronouncing forgiveness is rather presumptuous, insensitive even, to the offended party. In forgiving sins, Jesus is saying that he is not some unconnected third party but the one sinned against, namely God. He is the only one that can forgive all our sins because they are all ultimately committed against him (Psalm 51:4; Isaiah 43:25).

Now, the idea that we need God to forgive our sins can provoke a big reaction. While some take heart, others take offence. First, because of the implication that we have done things that need forgiving, and second, because we need God to forgive us. Some people think they can make amends and wipe out their guilt by doing good things: the good outweighing the bad. Others look to reincarnation, hoping (or dreading) to pay for their misdeeds in another life and have another go at doing things right. Still others look for salvation in statistics arguing, "I am better than most people, so I'm not really bad." The truth is, however, that we all need to hear Jesus say, "Take heart child, your sins are forgiven."

But wait a minute, it's easy to sympathise with the scribes' reaction, isn't it? Anyone can go round saying your sins are forgiven. If it's true, it's the best thing you can hear, but if it's not, it's the worst. To be given false assurance of spiritual health, only to discover when you meet your maker that you are still guilty, would be nothing short of catastrophic.

Well, Jesus provides some pretty convincing evidence. He says in effect: "Yes, I know it's easy for me to say your sins are forgiven because there is no instantaneous verification of that fact. Let me, therefore, say something equally incredible but immediately visible." He then turns to the paralysed man, tells him to get up, and lo and behold—he gets up! Jesus has just signed his message of forgiveness with his supernatural signature.

I love the little added detail that the man "went home". Can you picture the scene? The religious scoffers are standing there open-mouthed, and the crowd would be going wild as this man tucks his mat under his arm and strolls off home. I like to imagine him briefly catching the eyes of the scribes and giving them a little smile and a flick of his eyebrows as if to say, "Hey guys, guess you were wrong. My sins really are forgiven." The narrative, of course, stays with Jesus who goes on to invite Matthew, the writer of this account, to follow him. I would love to have heard more though about what happened when this ex-paralytic walked in through the front door of his house. I'm sure his family would have taken him seriously when he told them that his sins had been forgiven.

PETER AND PAUL PROVE IT TOO

Jesus often backed up his words with supernatural signs, and so did his disciples. He sent them out to preach a message and perform miraculous signs that confirmed it:

> They went out and preached everywhere, while the Lord worked with them and confirmed the message by accompanying signs. (Mark 16:20)

And that's the way it continued. As we shall see later on, after getting into trouble for preaching the gospel on the back of a healing miracle, Jesus' disciples pray:

> Lord ... enable your servants to speak your word with great boldness while you stretch out your hand to heal, and perform miraculous signs and wonders through the name of your holy servant Jesus. (Acts 4:29–30)

The book of Acts makes it clear that God answered that prayer. People listened to Peter when he preached the gospel because he healed the sick (Acts 9:34–35), and when he raised a woman from the dead the effect on the population of Joppa was pretty predictable:

> Peter put them all outside, and knelt down and prayed; and turning to the body he said, "Tabitha, arise." And she opened her eyes, and when she saw Peter she sat up. And he gave her his hand and raised her up. Then calling the saints and widows, he presented her alive. And it became known throughout all Joppa, and many believed in the Lord. (Acts 9:40–42)

Supernatural signs also accompanied Paul and Barnabas when they preached the gospel:

> They remained for a long time [at Iconium], speaking boldly for the Lord, who bore witness to the word of his grace, granting signs and wonders to be done by their hands. (Acts 14:3)

For Paul, the gospel is preached by weak people but demonstrated with God's power:

> For I decided to know nothing among you except Jesus Christ and him crucified. And I was with you in weakness and in fear and much trembling, and my

speech and my message were not in plausible words of wisdom, but in demonstration of the Spirit and of power. (1 Corinthians 2:2–4)

Paul's authority was evidenced by what he did:

The signs of a true apostle were performed among you with utmost patience, with signs and wonders and mighty works. (2 Corinthians 12:11–12)

The writer to the Hebrews knew that miracles accompanied the gospel when he wrote that salvation:

… was declared at first by the Lord, and it was attested to us by those who heard, while God also bore witness by signs and wonders and various miracles and by gifts of the Holy Spirit distributed according to his will. (Hebrews 2:3–4)

I have heard people say many times that faith is "believing in the absence of evidence" or even "believing in spite of the evidence". That simply is not true. The whole of Christianity and the gospel stands or falls on an event that took place in history: a massively miraculous sign that was performed to authenticate who Jesus was and what he said. Jesus made the prediction that he would be put to death and then be raised to life—a prediction that could be proved true or false by the subsequent turn of events:

Jesus began to show his disciples that he must go to Jerusalem and suffer many things from the elders and chief priests and scribes, and be killed, and on the third day be raised. (Matthew 16:21)

When that actually happened it added a huge amount of evidence to Jesus' claim to be the Son of God, come to earth to pay for our sins and give us new life. Jesus' resurrection was so important that he made sure there was good evidence for it:

> After his suffering, he showed himself to [people] and gave many convincing proofs that he was alive. (Acts 1:3)

This evidence was so significant to Jesus' first apostles that, when they came to replace Judas, they looked for someone who was a witness with them, not only to all that Jesus had done, but specifically to his resurrection (Acts 1:22).

CHURCH HISTORY

So the gospel has a supernatural sign at its heart, and in the Bible its proclamation was accompanied by supernatural signs, especially healing. Jesus said, "these signs will accompany those who believe; … they will lay hands on the sick, and they will recover" (Mark 16:17–18). That was certainly the case in the book of Acts, but what about in the second and third centuries? Did it continue?

Well, in the second century we find Justin Martyr (AD 100–165) writing about Christians healing people and Irenaeus (AD 125–200), a student of Polycarp who was a disciple of the apostle John, records that Christians:

> … still heal the sick by laying their hands upon them, and they are made whole … Yea, moreover, as I have said, the dead even have been raised up, and remain among us for many years. (Irenaeus, Against Heresies, Book 2, Volume 1, Chapter 32)

Tertullian (AD 160–240), an influential leader and apologist of the Western Church writes in a letter:

> How many men of rank (to say nothing of common

people) have been delivered from devils, and healed of diseases! (Tertullian, To Scapula, Chapter 4)

Origen (AD 185–284), the son of a martyred believer and the first systematic theologian, testified that signs and wonders were still accompanying Christians:

> Some give evidence of their having received through this faith a marvellous power by the cures which they perform, invoking no other name over those who need their help than that of the God of all things, and of Jesus, along with a mention of his history. (Origen, Against Celsus, Book 3, Chapter 24)

Novatian (AD 210–280), Bishop of Rome, recorded that the Holy Spirit:

> places prophets in the church, instructs teachers, directs tongues, gives powers and healings, does wonderful works. (Novatian, A Treatise of Novatian Concerning the Trinity, Chapter 29)

Many today still share the gospel this way. They heal the sick, cast out demons, and ask people to receive Jesus as their Lord and Saviour. People like Heidi Baker, Rienhard Bonnke, Bill Johnson, and thousands of other less well known, but equally faithful men and women, continue to do what Jesus did.

It's interesting to note people's reaction when the paralysed man gets up and walks home. They were "afraid and gave glory to God" (Matthew 9:8). Basically they began to take Jesus seriously. He had just stepped out of the box they had put him in, and there were some big implications for their life. Suddenly they became aware not only of their sin, but of God's presence, and the two don't mix well!

We can spend much of our lives trying to ignore God and our guilt, but when a paralysed man gets up from his mat and walks home, all the layers of self-justification and excuses, all the arguments that God is distant or a delusion, can fall away in a moment.

You can hear that "Jesus died for your sin to save you from hell and bring you back into a relationship with God", and it can sound like just another "belief". "You believe that, but I believe something else. So what?" But when you see someone healed in the name of Jesus, it can change everything. Suddenly the gospel becomes a whole lot more real and relevant, and this is as true today as it was in the first century.

EXTRATERRESTRIAL VISITORS

I want you to imagine a Martian coming down from outer space. His one eye looks around from atop its flexible stalk and focuses on a Bible. His long, lime green forefinger sucks open the front cover, and he begins to read. When he has finished, he hops off to look for a genuine "chuuuuurch" (Ever since Steven Spielberg's ET, I have imagined Martians talk that way).

What criteria will he use to find one? Well, surely he would look for a community of people who were worshipping Jesus, loving one another, and proclaiming the gospel, but would he not also be looking for a generous sprinkling of miracles? Surely we would not be surprised to find him looking for the hallmark of healing? If he found a group of people who loved each other but had no power to heal the sick, it might be rather hard to explain to him that it was, in fact, a real church (Mark 16:17, 18).

Now, I don't want to overstate the case, nor imply that a church without signs and wonders is not genuine, but I do want to highlight the massively miraculous way Jesus and the early church worked.

We need to reach for fruit in supernatural healing, not just because we care about those in the church who are terribly ill, but because we care about those outside the church, who are looking for marks of authenticity. Healing can help tip the scales of scepticism and expose the lie of anti-supernaturalism. People need to see that the offer of divine forgiveness is genuine. They need to see that the invisible and eternal things are not totally disconnected from the visible and temporal. They are in fact understandably, legitimately, and biblically looking for the hallmark of healing.

QUESTIONS

1) How were other people involved in bringing you to faith in Jesus? What can you do this week to bring others closer to Jesus?

2) What do you have faith for God to do today and in the weeks ahead? How will your actions be different because of that?

3) Have you seen someone being healed or, have you been healed yourself? What effect did it have on you or others?

4) What can you do that will help authenticate the gospel as you seek to tell people about Jesus?

5. THE TOUCH OF HEALING

"lay your hand on her, and she will live",
"If I only touch his garment, I will be made well."
Matthew 9:18, 21

A FINAL PASSAGE

We are now going to look at the last passage in Matthew's compendium of healing miracles. As we do so, I want to highlight some of the things we have seen so far as well as discover in it something new. To that end, we will consider three similarities in the lives of two people:

> While he was saying these things to them, behold, a ruler came in and knelt before him, saying, "My daughter has just died, but come and lay your hand on her, and she will live." And Jesus rose and followed him, with his disciples. And behold, a woman who had suffered from a discharge of blood for twelve years came up behind him and touched the fringe of his garment, for she said to herself, "If I only touch his garment, I will be made well." Jesus turned, and seeing her he said, "Take heart, daughter; your faith has made you well." And instantly the woman was made well.

> And when Jesus came to the ruler's house and saw the flute players and the crowd making a commotion, he said, "Go away, for the girl is not dead but sleeping." And they laughed at him. But when the crowd had been put outside, he went in and took her by the hand, and the girl arose. And the report of this went through all that district. (Matthew 9:18–26)

1. BOTH GET HEALED

I love watching 3D films. When done well, they make everything seem more vivid and real. The technology works by presenting a slightly different image to each eye, enabling our brain to calculate depth information. When it does so, objects seem to stand out from the screen in a way not possible in conventional 2D films. In a similar way, this passage is about two apparently unconnected people, a girl and a woman, but their stories are intertwined, and it seems to me that Matthew wants us to see them both together and appreciate something of the depth of God's desire to heal.

The first similarity in the lives of these two people is that they both get healed. In this short passage, Jesus heals not just one but two people. It reminds me of a shot in snooker called a "double". It's when you knock a ball onto the far cushion at such an angle that it rebounds into the opposite pocket. Well, Jesus is doing the supernatural equivalent here. He's on his way to raise a girl from the dead, when he bumps into a sick woman. She gets healed, then he goes on to raise the girl from the dead. Quite an impressive shot, I think you'll agree, and once again we get the impression that Jesus loves healing people and is rather good at it too!

While we are on the subject of sport, imagine with me for a moment that God was really into competitive sport; that it was in his nature to win, to compete, to challenge, and to push himself further and faster. If sport was at the core of who God was, and he decided to become a man, then this passage would read very differently:

> One day Jesus was out jogging with his disciples. A man approached him and begged him to join the Jerusalem City Rovers. On the way to his first game, Jesus got drawn into a cricket match. He scored a century, but by the time he arrived for the football match his side were down 2–0 with only sixty seconds left on the clock. With the opposing fans jeering and doing their best to put him off, he scored a hat-trick just before the final whistle. Everyone clapped and was inspired to play a lot more sport.

Matthew would have included in his gospel a passage on golf, a passage on tennis, and a passage on snooker, but he doesn't, does he? Instead, he has passage after passage about healing. That is because God loves to heal.

The book of Hebrews tells us that in the past God spoke to men at various times and in various ways but that now he has spoken to us by his Son (Hebrews 1:1–2). Looking at Jesus, we see a God who unquestionably loves to heal. Healing is his name (Exodus 15:26), and "healing is his game" (so to speak). This was the first thing that struck me when I read through chapters 8 and 9 of Matthew's gospel. As I did so, I realised just how into healing Jesus really was and how much his followers should be too. Are we more into healing than football or cricket? Do we prioritise it over TV and Facebook? I hope so!

2. BOTH HAD TO WAIT

The second similarity between the two stories is that they both had to wait. The woman had been ill for twelve years, and the little girl died before Jesus got to her.

We live in a universe, not only of space, but of time. Therefore, God's plan of salvation, his rescue and restoration, is working out in time and over time. As his glory is painted on a space-time canvas things happen in different places at different times. Since that is the way it is, we experience God's kingdom as both now and not yet. We live in the glorious outworking in time of God's eternal purposes in Christ.

I was not a Christian for twenty-four years of my life. I heard the gospel for years and didn't respond. Then one day I got it. I don't know why it took years, but I'm glad my friends and family were persistent. If I think twenty-four years was a long time to wait, what about Abraham and others, like Isaac and Moses, in the Old Testament?

They died believing promises that would only be fulfilled thousands of years later with the coming of Jesus (Hebrew 11:39). Yet all through their life they did not give up on God's goodness and faithfulness but trusted his promises and "greeted them from afar" (Hebrews 11:13).

I find this concept of welcoming God's promises from a distance so helpful. It reminds me of my children, when they were young, waiting for their cousins to arrive. They got so excited about it and kept asking, "When will they be here?" They knew that they were coming and were so looking forward to it, but any delay did not discourage them; rather, it revved up their eager anticipation to new heights. They looked out of the window, listened for the noise of a car drawing up, and rushed to answer the doorbell when it rang. In the same way, when you see a dear friend coming down the drive to your house you open the door, wave and call out to them, beckoning them in.

This is what these Old Testament heroes of faith did. They recognised that there was a distance between their current experience and God's promises, yet they could see their fulfilment coming down the road and engaged with it joyfully, calling and waving and beckoning. This is the opposite of becoming bitter and disappointed. How much more should we, who live on the other side of the cross, see and welcome the coming kingdom of God?

The woman and the girl had been ill for a long time and yet, when Jesus came, they took hold of him. The woman pressed through the crowd, and the girl's father sought Jesus out. It's plain by their actions that they hadn't lost hope in God. Perhaps you have been sick for a very long time or are hoping and praying for some great miracle in the life of a loved one but so far have not seen it. How can we keep our eyes on Jesus through such times and be ready to take hold of him when the time comes?

When we set out at the beginning of Matthew chapters 8 and 9, we conceptualised our journey as one of experience and expectation. We wanted to be honest about our current experience and yet faithful to a biblical expectation. As we do this, we are living in the gap, and that's where this woman had been for twelve long years. To live in the gap, we need to keep experience and expectation in balance and make sure that we do not focus on one to the detriment of the other.

We need to keep our eyes on our experience for at least three reasons. The first is so that we can care for people. There is a danger when we fix our sights on miraculous healing that we can take our eyes off Spirit-empowered caring. In looking for instant healing, we can forget about long-term helping. You see, instant miracles go hand in hand with on-going mercy, and signs and wonders should take place in the context of compassion and kindness. As we focus on raising our expectation for healing, therefore, we need to excel in on-going support for those who have not yet been healed. Our motivation to see people supernaturally healed also compels us to care for those who are not. Perhaps you can think of something right now that you could do to show practical care and love to someone who is unwell.

Even if you are not well yourself, please don't exclude yourself from the privilege of serving others in this way. We can care and pray for people even while we are seeking God for healing ourselves. Your own suffering may even give you a greater understanding and compassion for others. I remember fondly one particular lady who, though very seriously ill herself, would always get in first with her kind enquiries as to my comparatively minor ailments. I found her concern deeply touching. However ill we are, we need to remember that our identity is not in our current state of health but in Christ, and we should act out of that, remembering that God loves to display his power in weakness.

There is a second reason, though, why we need to keep an eye on what is actually going on around us. If I am honest, sometimes I can be tempted to close my eyes to the pain and challenges of this world to protect my wavering faith, but that is not how real faith works. Trying to protect your faith like this is akin to keeping a fish out of water in case it drowns. Now, there is a false faith, a stunted immature faith, a natural faith, that can't survive when it looks at things that challenge it. It is easily overcome by disappointment and rarely returns to fight another day. True faith, on the other hand, is very resilient. Its nature is to look at disappointments and setbacks and say, "This will change. This must change!" It rises stronger than before from the ashes of apparent defeat with renewed conviction and determination.

It's like when the hero gets punched in an action movie. Slowly they wipe the corner of their mouth with the back of their hand. With great measure and control they look at it to confirm that their assailant has indeed dared to draw blood. A steely look comes into their eyes, as if to say, "You are really going to regret that. I've been holding back, being nice to you, but now I'm about to get serious and take this fight to a whole other level."

Imagine a drill bit that looks sharp and strong but blunts and bends the minute you press it into something hard. When you take it back to the shop you are told it's only supposed to be used on soft things like butter, but who needs a drill bit to cut through dairy products? Anything can do that. My finger can do that. True faith is like a diamond-tipped steel drill bit that keeps its point even when being ground into hard granite.

Authentic, supernatural faith gets up from a fall and presses on again because it is based on knowing God and his unchangeable word. It sets its course through the foggy darkness using a compass that always points towards the love, power, and faithfulness of God, in Jesus Christ. For the Christian, Christ is true north, and he always orientates us in the direction of healing.

Let me illustrate the tenacious nature of faith in one last way. I used to play rugby at school, and one of the best bits for me was the scrum. Each team locks together to form a human bulldozer, and then both muscle machines crunch into one another to take the strain. A ball is placed in the middle, and you try to push the other team back so it can be picked up by your team and driven forward. No one in a scrum is surprised that the other side pushes back; rather, they are strengthened in their resolve to win.

For a few seconds there is a lot of grunting as studs dig in and adrenaline builds up. The moment you sense the resolve of the other side wavering, just a fraction, is key. You can't see it from outside, but you can feel it from within. You let out a roar, dig deep, and draw on hidden reserves to push forward for victory.

Faith should be like a rugby scrum, but sometimes we don't even stick around to take up the strain. We need to stand our ground and push even if we don't seem to be getting anywhere. True faith refuses to give ground and then pushes forward to drive home the kingdom of God.

The third reason we need to keep our eyes on our experience is so that we can share testimonies of what God is doing. Faith doesn't get discouraged by stories of what God isn't doing, but it is encouraged by testimonies of what he is doing. In fact, faith has a pen in its hand ready to write more! I have been in many situations where a story of healing is shared and someone gets healed off the back of it. I wonder how many stories of Jesus healing people had reached the ears of the sick woman and the little girl's family. I bet those accounts would have increased their faith as Jesus drew near. They had certainly taken the strain over the years and were ready to push through when they heard that Jesus was in town.

While there are some good reasons to keep one eye on our experience, there are also good reasons to keep the other on the Bible, and this is perhaps the thing we find hardest. You see, we are not just to be ministers of mercy but workers of miracles. That is why time spent studying these particular passages is time well spent.

In John's gospel, after raising a girl to life, Jesus goes on to say that those who believe in him will do greater things (John 14:12). Take a moment to let that recalibrate your expectation. What is your current expectation? What are you expecting to see today? This week? This year? In your lifetime? This year I am expecting to hear many testimonies of people being healed. In my lifetime, I'm expecting to see people healed of multiple sclerosis, cancer, paralysis, and even, raised from the dead.

When Jesus came to raise the girl from the dead, some laughed (Matthew 9:24). We must not let years of waiting wear down our faith. We must not, like Abraham's wife, think that God is against us or holding out on us (Genesis 16:2). She began to speak and act, not out of the promises of God, but out of her own thoughts and ideas. When the time comes for God to act, we don't want to be those who laugh (Genesis 18:12). Do you laugh at the idea of people getting miraculously healed? What about people getting raised from the dead? For some it's not a loud, audible laugh but a deeper, silent, and cynical, "Yeah, right." The father of the girl and the woman with the bleeding didn't laugh. They heard, they believed, and then they saw.

3. BOTH GOT TOUCHED

We come now to the final similarity we are going to look at, and it will be something fresh for us to wield in our battle. Let's go to Mark's gospel for a change and see how Jesus heals people there.

When a leper came to Jesus asking to be made clean, Jesus "stretched out his hand and *touched* him … And immediately the leprosy left him" (Mark 1:40–42). Those who had diseases pressed around Jesus "to *touch* him" (Mark 3:10). People asked about Jesus, "How are such mighty works done by his *hands?*" (Mark 6:2). In his hometown, Jesus "laid his *hands* on a few sick people and healed them" (Mark 6:5–6). Wherever he went, sick people "implored him that they might *touch* even the fringe of his garment. And as many as *touched* it were made well." (Mark 6:56).

When people brought a deaf man with a speech impediment to Jesus, "They begged him to lay his *hand* on him … And his ears were opened, his tongue was released, and he spoke plainly" (Mark 7:32, 35). When Jesus was in Bethsaida "some people brought to him a blind man and begged him to *touch* him" (Mark 8:22). After Jesus spat on his eyes and laid *hands* on him twice, "his sight was restored, and he saw everything clearly" (Mark 8:22–25).

Time and time again Jesus' touch releases healing power into people's lives. Luke records it too:

> Now when the sun was setting, all those who had any who were sick with various diseases brought them to him, and he laid his hands on every one of them and healed them. (Luke 4:40)

Jesus' touch was so powerful it raised the dead:

> … he came up and touched the bier (coffin NIV), and the bearers stood still. And he said, "Young man, I say

to you, arise." And the dead man sat up and began to speak, and Jesus gave him to his mother. (Luke 7:12–15)

Even when he was being arrested, his touch brought healing:

One of them struck the servant of the high priest and cut off his right ear. But Jesus said, "No more of this!" And he touched his ear and healed him. (Luke 22:50–51)

Finally, in Matthew's gospel just before our current passage:

And when Jesus entered Peter's house, he saw his mother-in-law lying sick with a fever. He touched her hand, and the fever left her, and she rose and began to serve him. (Matthew 8:14–15)

When Jesus heals people, he often touches them and, indeed, in our current passage that is exactly how Jesus was expected to heal both the woman and the girl. The father said to Jesus, "Come and lay your hand on her, and she will live" (Matthew 9:18), and the woman said to herself, "If only I touch his garment I will be made well" (Matthew 9:21). Later on, two blind men call out to Jesus:

… "Lord, let our eyes be opened." And Jesus in pity touched their eyes, and immediately they recovered their sight and followed him. (Matthew 20:33–34)

It is clear that Jesus' touch brought healing. Interestingly enough, there is even a hint that it brought emotional healing too:

He was still speaking when, behold, a bright cloud overshadowed them, and a voice from the cloud said, "This is my beloved Son, with whom I am well pleased;

listen to him." When the disciples heard this, they fell on their faces and were terrified. But Jesus came and touched them, saying, "Rise, and have no fear." (Matthew 17:5–7)

A FLOW OF HEALING POWER

So what happens when people come into physical contact with Jesus? Well, when the woman touches Jesus he turns round to see who touched him. The crowd is pressing in all round him, yet he notices a woman touch the tip of a tassel on the hem of his garment. Luke's account tells us why, when Jesus says:

> Someone touched me, for I perceive that power has gone out from me. (Luke 8:46)

Power emanated from Jesus. It flowed from him. Luke says of a previous time:

> All the crowd sought to touch him, for power came out from him and healed them all. (Luke 6:19)

Every time someone touched Jesus in faith, or he touched them with compassion, there was a flow of power from the heart of God. In contrast to the leper's touch, which was thought to bring death, Jesus' touch brought life, and so can the touch of his followers.

What sign did Jesus say would accompany those who believed in him? It was this: "… they will lay their hands on the sick and they will recover" (Mark 16:18). If you have put your trust in Jesus as your Lord and Saviour, accepting his death on the cross as payment for your sin and determining to follow him, then you are a temple of the Holy Spirit (1 Corinthians 6:18–20): a physical dwelling place for God. Jesus, therefore, is present in you by his Spirit. The implications of that are huge, and we will spend the rest of our lives getting our heads round it. For now, though, I just want to highlight the fact that we are a conduit and carrier for the healing power of Jesus.

I hesitate to use the word "channel" because it is often associated with counterfeit powers of healing. With the genuine there is often the counterfeit, and healing is no exception. The challenge is for the church to so shine with this hallmark that the dim and tarnished nature of the counterfeit is shown up. Pharaoh's magicians could replicate some of the plagues, but they got left behind in the power game pretty early on (Exodus 7:22; 8:7, 18). Elijah did not shy away from going head to head with the prophets of Baal (1 Kings 18:21–40) but raised the stakes knowing his God was infinitely stronger. Jesus is way more powerful than any other power and it should show.

You might want to take a look at your hands right now. If you are a Christian they are not just for peeling potatoes, putting on plasters, or even for performing open-heart surgery. Those are all good things, and God can work powerfully through them, but he also wants you to supernaturally heal people with those hands.

When someone's heart stops, medics rush in with a piece of equipment called a defibrillator. Two metal discs are placed on the patient's chest, and an electrical current is passed through them to jump-start the heart. When you place your hands on non-functioning bodies, the Holy Spirit can flow through you and get things working again. God really can use your hands to jump-start eyes, ears, and limbs.

A SHOPPING SPREE

Having looked at chapters 8 and 9 of Mathew's gospel, it is clear that Jesus was really into healing (sorry to labour the point but Matthew does too). We also looked at Jesus' authority. Just as the centurion's orders were backed up by the might of Rome, so Jesus' orders are backed up by the might of heaven. Since Jesus gave authority to his disciples "to heal every disease" (Matthew 10:1), the power of heaven is ready to back you up when you step out.

Helpfully, Matthew points to the cross as the place where Jesus dealt with our sickness by quoting from the prophet Isaiah speaking hundreds of years earlier:

> Surely he took our illnesses and bore our diseases.
> (Isaiah 53:4)

Healing has already been purchased. Imagine you were given ten thousand pounds credit to spend at your local superstore. Someone else has earned the money and given it to you. All you need to do is go down there, grab a trolley, and fill it up. Well, we have been given massive credit to spend in extending the kingdom of heaven, so why not go on a spending spree?

We have also seen how Jesus does far more than simply heal people. In fact, healing is a mark of authority for, the less immediately visible but far greater work of, forgiveness and reconciliation. Healing is the hallmark of the gospel: the good news that you can be forgiven by God through faith in Jesus Christ. Jesus' disciples shared the gospel with people and continued to stamp it with the hallmark of healing.

Finally, in this chapter, we finished by highlighting one of the key ways in which God's healing power flows through Jesus, and through us, to people who are hurt and broken. God made us physical beings with the ability to connect not just through words, but also through touch. As we lay our hands on sick people, the power of God at work in us gets to work on them too.

QUESTIONS

1) Do you know anybody who is currently unwell? Are there any practical ways that you can help them?

2) How can your own struggles and challenges with ill health motivate and equip you to bring healing to others?

3) How have setbacks and disappointments affected (either positively or negatively) your faith for people to be healed?

4) Take a look at your hands. Given that the Holy Spirit is in you, what does God want you to do with those hands?

PART II
THE HEALING POWER OF JESUS
IN ACTS

INTRODUCTION TO PART II

In Part I we looked at a number of the healing miracles of Jesus as recorded by one of his disciples. We have seen that Jesus' compassion not only led him to heal people, but to bring them into an eternal life-giving relationship with his Father. Both of these things were purchased by Jesus on the cross and administered through his words and touch.

If we read the rest of Matthew's gospel and continue on into the book of Acts, we find that pretty soon after Jesus commands his disciples to preach the gospel and heal the sick, he leaves! They are left open-mouthed looking up into the sky because Jesus' absence represents for them a massive change in circumstances. He healed while he was on earth and, to an extent, so did his disciples, but when he goes it's like the plug being pulled on a heavy metal rock band. It's no good having loud speakers that go up to eleven without the power to drive them. So with Jesus no longer physically around, is it the end of supernatural healing? Does the church go acoustic?

How are we to advance and demonstrate the kingdom of God now that Jesus has gone? How do we build the church, preach the gospel, and introduce people to Jesus when he is not physically around? Do we do things another way, follow another example, or devise another strategy? We will answer these questions here in Part II by looking at Acts, the book in the New Testament that Luke starts with the enigmatic phrase:

> In the first book, O Theophilus, I have dealt with all
> that Jesus began to do and teach. (Acts 1:1)

As many have pointed out, the author's clear implication is that after his ascension Jesus continues to act powerfully in and through the church. But just how is that possible? How does that work, and how can we release his power today?

As I started looking for answers in the book of Acts, I discovered that many miraculous signs were done by the apostles (Acts 5:12). My plan, therefore, was to go through them all, one at a time, as I had done with the healing miracles of Jesus in Matthew's gospel. The Holy Spirit, however, had a better idea. Unsuspectingly, I worked hard on a six point message based on the first healing miracle in the book of Acts.

At around midnight on Saturday, it dawned on me that I had far too much material. It's not usually very helpful to get half way through a message and have to rush the rest because of time, so I did something radical: I decided that I would just see how far I got on the day. I was expecting to cover at least two points, but as it was I finished only one. In the next message, when I only got through one more point, I began to get the idea that I should stay on this first miracle for the rest of the series.

There is so much we can learn from this one miracle alone that will help us obey Jesus' command to heal the sick. Peter and John saw the power of Jesus released in their community, and so can we. Before we begin to look at this healing, why not take a couple of minutes to read Acts chapters 3 and 4 to get a feel for this incredible story? As you do so, think about how it relates to some of the things we have already learnt from the life of Jesus.

1. SEIZE THE MOMENT

"looking at him"
Acts 3:4

AZUSA STREET

Having looked at how Jesus healed a number of people in Matthew chapters 8 and 9, we are now moving on to look at how Jesus' disciples began to do the same in Acts chapters 3 and 4. Let's just remind ourselves of the story: Jesus has ascended to heaven, the Holy Spirit has been poured out, and the disciples have begun to preach the gospel with accompanying supernatural phenomena, including healing. We are going to be looking in detail at the first recorded healing after Jesus' ascension where a man, lame from birth, jumps to his feet.

It's important to realise that the events recorded in the book of Acts do not represent the high point of God's power being exerted on the earth; they are just the start. What we read in Acts 3 and 4 is not a blip but the ball beginning to roll. It puts me in mind of the start of a Formula One race, with the whine and buzz of supercharged engines playing the scale of "insane acceleration" through their gear boxes.

Sometimes church history and modern day experience makes it look like the red flag has been waved, suspending the race and forcing everyone to cruise slowly and carefully round the track without overtaking, but Jesus has done no such thing. The baptism of fire that John the Baptist talked about was not just for those first century Christians at the front of the queue. The source of the fire that came down on them has not been extinguished but has burnt a glorious trail through history, right up to the present day. The race is still very much on!

One highlight was about hundred years ago when God started showing up in a dirty warehouse in LA. As Christians met to pray and seek God at Azusa Street, a cloud would often appear, and amazing miracles would happen in the name of Jesus. Cancers would drop off, people would get out of wheelchairs, and missing limbs would grow back. A few times, the fire brigade was even called when people reported seeing flames coming up from the roof and down from the sky, and at such times, the greatest miracles tended to happen.

I don't know how you feel when you read these things, but the more I read the Bible, the more normal these accounts sound to me. It is puzzling, therefore, when people don't get healed. As I live in the gap between my current experience and a biblically based expectation, I am encouraged when I look in my rear view mirror and see things like Azusa Street. Hearing about them makes me long for, and look forward to, more and greater moves of God.

Interestingly enough, in 1909, William Seymour, the leader of the Azusa street gathering, prophesied that around hundred years later there would be an even greater visitation of God all over the world. One has to weigh these things of course, but these are certainly exciting times to be living in. Moves of God around the world are catching my attention and stirring hope. Are you thirsty? I am! I long for revival, but there is a danger with that longing if it leads to passivity. We are not to wait but to weigh in. What's the point of waiting until the fire is lit to strike a match?

Whether we are in a time of revival or not, God wants us to step out now, so let's continue to look at God's word, and let it stir us to faith for all that he wants to do in our generation. We have looked at Jesus healing people; now let's look at the first recorded healing miracle by his disciples in Acts chapters 3 and 4.

SQUIRREL!

In the Pixar movie "UP", the mad explorer Charles Muntz attaches special collars to his dogs which translate their barks into English. This means we get to listen in on their conversations as they carry out their master's evil commands. What's interesting (and funny) is that, every now and then, their serious discussion is temporarily disrupted when one of them shouts "Squirrel!" At that point, they all suddenly sit bolt upright with eyes locked onto something off screen. For a time, nothing else matters as the irrepressible instincts of their canine brains take charge. A few seconds later, the moment passes, and they pick up their conversation where they had left off.

The account of Peter and John in Acts 3 reminds me of those moments in the film. They are walking along, talking about this and that, when a man calls out to them asking for money. It's as if Peter shouts, "Squirrel!", and both he and John lock eyes on this man for the next few minutes. It's a "God moment" where something special is about to happen.

We need to be alert to these moments when they come along and seize them. They need to capture our attention like the slightest rustle in the bushes alerts a dog to the potential presence of a squirrel. Let's look at some of the characteristics of this moment so we don't miss them in our own lives.

First, notice that it's in a normal, everyday context. Peter and John are just doing what they must have done dozens of times before: going up to the temple to pray. It's in just such ordinary places that God wants to do extraordinary things, not in special or faraway places, but in our everyday lives; it can happen in the office, at the school gate, or in a coffee shop.

Second, it must have been a bit inconvenient for them. Peter and John are on their way to a meeting "at the time of prayer". The man calls out to them for money, but they have an appointment and don't want to be late. Like many such moments, the timing is not convenient. We are busy carrying out our plans when God breaks in with his. At such times we need to be flexible. God's plans are always much better anyway.

Third, they are thinking out of the box. The man is asking for money, but Peter and John don't have any. They could have said, "Sorry, we can't help" and carried on, but they were aware of a bigger picture.

Sometimes people ask for second best because they have lost hope for first best. They are stuck in a box, and the lid is firmly shut. They ask for what would help them rather than what would heal them, for relief of their symptoms rather than removal of the cause. This man had no hope of getting his mobility back and, therefore, no chance to earn a living. He was reduced to begging for money to buy food to keep himself alive. Peter, on the other hand, lived outside of that particular box with a God who could give someone their legs back.

Many times people ask for money, friendship, cars, status, drink, drugs, or whatever because they have given up on first best. Inner peace has become a pipe dream, overflowing joy a lost cause. They think that the best that can be done with guilt and shame is to drown it out with frantic activity, or numb it with addictive narcotics. People silently learn to live with the wrong done to them until they can bear it no longer. Some think that being loved perfectly forever and living happily ever after only happens in chick-flicks, and as for death, well, we all die one day so let's make the most of life while we can. This is what it's like living in a box, but we need to think and breathe outside of the box in the kingdom of God where the lame walk, the blind see, and the deaf hear. To do that, we need to be immersed in God's word and keep close to Jesus the King.

That's why it is so good to spend time reading Matthew 8 and 9, and Acts 3 and 4. It gets us out of the box of yesterday's disappointments, out of the bin-liner of scientific naturalism, and out of the bag of plain old unbelief. Let's think and live outside in the wide open space of the kingdom of heaven.

WHY NOW?

So, Peter and John were expecting the kingdom of God to break out in ordinary situations—but why now, at this particular point in time?

Firstly, it could be because they saw this man's faith for healing. That does happen in Acts 14:9, and Jesus often looked for and responded to people's faith (Matthew 9:2). I'm not so sure that it is the deciding factor in this case, however; the faith in operation seems to be primarily that of Peter and John. I hope I am not doing this man an injustice, but it seems to me that he was just after their money.

Secondly, it could be that God had given them a bit of a heads-up. He could have said to them previously, "There will be a guy sitting on the ground by the temple gate wearing a red baseball cap. He will ask you for money, and that will be a sign that I am going to heal him." God does do that. After all, Jesus appeared in a vision to a man called Ananias and said:

> Rise and go to the street called Straight, and at the house of Judas look for a man of Tarsus named Saul, for behold, he is praying, and he has seen in a vision a man named Ananias come in and lay his hands on him so that he might regain his sight. (Acts 9:11–12)

That's pretty specific, don't you think? And it wasn't a one-off. According to Joel 2:28, the coming of the Spirit wasn't so that one man would see visions but that all people, men and women, both young and old, would be involved in all sorts of supernatural activity. We live in an age of prolific supernatural direction by the Spirit, so it's not a bad idea to start your day by asking God to show you want he wants to do through you. Ask him for clues and things to look out for.

Thirdly, God can speak into a situation at any time. He might have just said right there and then, "I'm going to heal that man." The Holy Spirit is always with us. He can suddenly say to us "that man" or "that woman", just like a security guard might get directions through an ear-piece. It may not be an audible voice but an inner feeling or a thought. Through familiarity with God's word, and trial and error, we can learn to distinguish his voice from our normal, internal babble.

Fourthly, Jesus says something very revealing before he raises Lazarus from the dead. He says, "Father, I thank you that you have heard me" (John 11:41), which strongly suggests that he had previously asked his Father to raise his friend from the dead. When the disciples can't heal someone, Jesus tells them that the key is prayer (Mark 9:29). Maybe they had learned that lesson well and had been up all night asking God to heal this guy.

Since God does speak to us about these things and he responds to our prayers, we must listen and ask, but here's the thing: Jesus didn't say when he sent his disciples off to heal the sick (Matthew 10:8) that they would have a specific word from God each time. He just said to go and do it. And they did.

There is a danger that in our eagerness to hear and obey God and to walk by the Spirit, we ignore or fail to obey what Jesus has already said. For example, we shouldn't wait for a specific word from God to get baptised as he has already told us to "Repent and be baptised" (Acts 2:38). We don't wait for a specific sign from heaven to help someone in need; Jesus has already told us, "Love your neighbour" (Luke 10:27–28). Similarly I don't need a prophetic word to love my wife or to share the gospel with a friend; I already have the green light for those things. I think the same applies when it comes to supernatural healing.

We need to be persuaded from the Bible that God can and will heal. The disciples had been with God incarnate for three years and witnessed him heal many hundreds of people. We are not told of any who went away still sick, and we are explicitly told on one occasion that he healed them all (Matthew 12:15).

MOVING GOD

The story of Gideon (Judges 6–8) encourages me that God is so gracious that he does often give us extra nudges and confirmations. However, we can confidently expect God to heal without seeing writing in the sky because we already have his word on the page. Faith can come from a prophetic word or a time of prayer, and we certainly want to cultivate and develop a relationship with the Holy Spirit in order to be sensitive to his impromptu promptings, but that must not lead us into passivity. It seems to me that the Bible gives us a default position that God will heal. In fact, it would take more than writing in the sky to persuade me otherwise, so clear is his word on the matter. This is important because it's easy to live as if the opposite is the case and, therefore, not expect God to heal a given person unless he explicitly tells us that he is going to.

Smith Wigglesworth was a man who knew God wanted to heal. He was reported to have said, "If God is not moving, I move him." By that, I don't think he meant that God was unwilling in any way or needed to be persuaded to do something; rather, that if God seemed not to be working specifically in a given situation where he has already expressed his will generally, like healing for example, then we should be confident and bold in stepping out and expecting him to show up. It may feel like we are making the first move but actually God did that years ago in the person of his son Jesus.

God has revealed enough of himself that we know he is willing and able to heal. If someone is not well, and we have no prophetic word, little sense of God's presence, and no encouragement from anybody that he is going to do anything, then we still have every reason to expect an amazing miracle—another God moment!

QUESTIONS

1) Are there any historical accounts of God moving supernaturally in the past that encourage you?

2) Have you ever had a "squirrel" moment when you knew that God was going to do something special? How did you know? Why not spend some time praying and asking God to give you some more?

3) Do you need a specific indication from God that he will heal an individual before you pray for them? Why is that?

2. HAVE THE CONFIDENCE

"look at us"
Acts 3:4

ON THE STREETS

We are looking at the first recorded healing miracle in the book of Acts in which Peter tells a lame man to get up. One of the things that stands out for me in this account, apart from the amazing nature of the miracle, is the huge confidence that Peter and John have. After recognising that this was a moment when God wanted to do something, Peter says in verse 4, "Look at us", and again in verse 6, "What I have I give to you." It reminds me of Christians who approach strangers on the street, start chatting to them, and then say something like "You have a problem with your shoulder, don't you?" When that turns out to be true, they say to any bystanders, "Gather round and watch this." After a quick prayer the shoulder gets better and everyone is amazed. I've seen that in larger settings too, where the speaker announces that God wants to heal people, and lo and behold he does, by the dozen! Peter and John, and others today, seem really confident that God will heal, but where does this kind of confidence come from?

THEY HAD SEEN JESUS HEAL

Well, as we have already noted, Peter and John had been with Jesus. They had seen him in action first-hand and knew full well what God was like. The fact that Jesus loved to heal people tells us that God loves to heal people (Colossians 2:9; Hebrews 1:2). That is why we have spent over half of this book looking at Jesus healing one person after another. We have read it, and they had seen it. It's good to get around people today who see lots of miracles happen as it reminds us that God is still in the business of healing people.

But just the fact that they had been around Jesus doesn't explain what they actually said. They didn't say "Look up there to Jesus in heaven", or even "Look over there at so and so", but "Look at us" (Acts 3:4). They are confident and expectant, not just that God wants to heal, but that he will work through them to do it. In fact, when they say "What I have I give to you", (Acts 3:6) it seems that they think God has already given them all that is needed to bring about this man's healing.

This is very significant and gets to the heart of what I want to look at in this part of the book. Jesus is physically in heaven, but he continues to do the things he did when he walked on the earth. He does them through ordinary men and women, not only like Peter and John, but also like you and me. That feels awkward because we know what we are like. I, like everybody else, am in daily need of the grace of God. I have mixed motives, limited ability and a patchy past—just like Peter and John in fact! It would be much easier to get someone to look elsewhere, but no, they say "Look at us."

So Jesus is in heaven, and he wants to work through us to heal, but there is still a missing piece of the puzzle that needs to be put in place in order for us to have the confidence to step out and expect God to back us up.

THE HOLY SPIRIT

The missing piece is actually a person and he is, of course, the Holy Spirit: the third person of the trinity. By starting at chapter 3 in Acts we have leapfrogged over the most important chapter in the whole book. Nothing we read in all of Acts will make much sense if we skip chapter 2. There we see that when Jesus goes to be with his Father in heaven, he receives and pours out the promised Holy Spirit (Luke 24:49; John 14:16–18; 16:7). In the torrential downpour, the timid disciples are swept out on to the streets to boldly do the things that Jesus did. Through men and women filled with the Holy Spirit, the power of Jesus is released again, not just in one place, but in a billion places all over the planet.

The Holy Spirit is the Christian's batteries, coach, guide, prompt, and power all rolled into one. What Jesus said to his disciples in Acts 1:4 before he left was basically like the old credit card slogan "Don't leave home without it." With the Spirit we have purchasing power to acquire territory for the kingdom of heaven.

VIVE LA DIFFERENCE

Don't underestimate the difference that the Holy Spirit made to these men. The description of the disciples after Jesus' departure at the end of chapter 1 is very revealing. They are doing a lot of good things. Instead of dispersing they have gathered together to pray (Acts 1:14; 2:1). They are placing a high value on God's word, studying it and seeking to apply it, plus they are giving proper attention to matters of internal structure such as the appointing of leaders (Acts 1:20). All well and good as far it goes, but it seems that some things are missing.

Firstly, there isn't the felt, experienced, and discernible presence of God among them. Being a Christian was being with Jesus, but now he had gone. They are responsive to the word but are casting lots to determine what God wants them to do. That's not necessarily wrong; it's just not very personal—a bit like "one knock for yes and two for no". God's spoken voice is absent, but a better way is coming.

Secondly, although they feel the responsibility for evangelism, it's not happening, and there is a total absence of mission. It's not a lack of obedience as Jesus has told them to wait, but they are not exactly chomping at the bit, and there is a strong smell of fear in the air. It's rather telling that when Jesus came to them after his resurrection the doors were locked "for fear of the Jews" (John 20:19), and when he came again to show himself to Thomas the doors were still bolted (John 20:26). They knew they should, and would, be witnesses to the resurrection, but they remained shut-in behind closed doors. That too was about to change.

It was Jesus' intention that his church should be biblical but not bookish, structured but not static. He wanted her to have a reverence for God, but not a remoteness from him, and to see mission as not just important, but urgent. The disciples, gathered in the upper room, were waiting, like a pile of dry wood before bonfire night, to be lit. This, Jesus did in style when he baptised them with the Holy Spirit and with fire.

HIGH EXPECTATIONS
When Jesus promised that they would receive the gift of the Spirit (Acts 1:4–5), Peter and John would have had a clear expectation of what that would entail. They would have grown up on the stories of David, Saul, Balaam, Samson, Othniel, Jephthah, Gideon, Moses, Joshua, Elisha, Elijah and others. When the Spirit came upon these Old Testament heroes they won victories, prophesied mysteries, lead armies, blew trumpets, dismembered lions, healed bodies, slew hundreds, and did all sorts of amazing miracles.

In the past, God's Spirit had come on special people for special tasks, but now his Spirit was to be on all God's people.

The prophets had looked forward to this day. Joel, Moses, Isaiah, and Ezekiel all glimpsed it, and Jesus had spoken about it too: a time when every believer was a special person commissioned with a special task. Peter and John, and all the other Christians, were now anointed with the Spirit: set apart and empowered to take the gospel to the nations. That could be next door or half way round the globe, but it can only be done, in the way God wants it to be done, when we are filled with the Holy Spirit. The Christian life is to be lived with power. The gospel comes with batteries included (Acts 2:38), and the church should have fire in its belly!

NOT A ONE-OFF
The experience of the early disciples was not a one-off, once-for-all event. As we read through the rest of Acts, one group of believers after another is filled with the Holy Spirit.

Philip preached the gospel in Samaria, did lots of miracles, and lots of people became Christians, but something was missing. They had not received the Holy Spirit. So Peter and John came down from Jerusalem to sort that out (Acts 8:14–17). The apostle Paul had an encounter with the risen Jesus on the road to Damascus but then had to go and find a guy called Ananias in order to receive the Spirit (Acts 9:17). Peter reported that when he preached to the gentiles at Cornelius' house (Acts 10:44–46) "the Holy Spirit fell on them just as on us at the beginning" (Acts 11:15). When Paul finds some disciples at Ephesus, his first question is "Did you receive the Holy Spirit when you believed?" (Acts 19:2). It turned out that they had not even been baptised in the name of Jesus, so Paul baptised them and then laid hands on them, at which point they received the Spirit.

Looking at these events it seems to me that receiving the Holy Spirit was experiential, visible, and often involved other people. Peter and John knew they had been given something, and they wanted to make sure that other Christians had it too.

No one need miss out. In fact, when Peter first preached the gospel he includes the promise of the Holy Spirit and made it explicitly clear that it was for everyone, everywhere:

> Repent and be baptised, every one of you, in the name of Jesus Christ for the forgiveness of your sins. And you will receive the gift of the Holy Spirit. For the promise is for you and for your children and for all who are far off, everyone whom the Lord our God calls to himself. (Acts 2:38–39)

The immediate context is significant because the crowd's expectation and understanding would not only have been shaped by the Old Testament people and prophets, but by the fact that they had just seen the disciples receive the Spirit.

Jesus had impressed upon Peter and John the importance of receiving the Holy Spirit, and they in turn helped others to receive it. In line with Jesus' own teaching, they would have built an expectation (Acts 1:4, 8) and made sure no one excluded themselves (John 7:39). They would have encouraged people to come to Jesus in faith (John 7:37, 38), ask the Father (Luke 11:13), and receive the Spirit (John 7:37).

We can sometimes struggle with actively receiving or "drinking" (John 4:10) the Spirit, but it simply involves joining in with the working of the Spirit as he comes to us. That might mean praising God, speaking in tongues, or even prophesying. I have personally found it helpful to enjoy and thank God for what he is already doing rather than be anxious about what he is not. Perhaps a Bible verse pops into your head, or the simple thought that God loves you "no matter what". Allow yourself to enjoy these things, even though they might seem small compared to the experience of others. Treasure them. Thank the Lord for what he is doing, and ask him to keep filling you with his Spirit and revealing more of his amazing love to you.

The Holy Spirit does not usually bypass our conscious decision making and waggle our tongues for us. Rather, he wants to work with us and alongside us. As we come to Jesus in faith, asking our Father for his Spirit, we may need to take the handbrake off our tongues a little and break the sound barrier. It's just the same when we pray for someone to be healed. We have to offer, then stretch out our hand, and speak healing in Jesus' name. As we do, the Holy Spirit is working with us and through us.

The Holy Spirit made all the difference to Peter and John. When you are drenched and filled with the Holy Spirit, when God is in you and all over you, when he has clothed you with power and put you on like a coat, I would say you are going to experience a measurable increase in confidence. Every situation you encounter then becomes an opportunity for the power of Jesus to be released.

A LIVING LINK

There are wires behind my TV. They are not there to be pretty. Personally I don't notice them but my wife does, and she says they are an unsightly mess. No matter how much I tie them up, they seem to get into a pickle again. Anyway, they are there to carry power and information to my TV, and it's the same with you and me. Right now, we are not here to look pretty, decorating the earth like hundreds and thousands sprinkled on a blob of ice cream. It's no good having our lives and our meetings nicely in order if there is no supernatural power to communicate the message we have been entrusted with. We must never forget we are here to deliver power and information to a dark and chaotic world.

The gospel needs to be articulated clearly and demonstrated powerfully, as Paul says, "not in words but with a demonstration of the Spirit's power" (1 Corinthians 2:4). The Christian is a conduit, a conductor, a living link between heaven and earth carrying God's word with God's power.

HE IS WITH YOU ALWAYS

We saw in the last chapter that we can be confident that God wants to heal. However, that is only half the battle. The other half is believing that he can and will do it through us. Knowing we have God with us and in us in the person of the Holy Spirit should give us great confidence as we step out.

Many years ago I did a one week residential course on theology and leadership. It was a great course, and I learnt a lot from it, but one thing really stuck in my mind. In a lecture on pastoring people, we had looked at all sorts of challenging situations like marriage breakdown, sickness, and death. At such times there seems to be little that can be said or done to help or comfort, but here's what the lecturer, a seasoned pastor himself, said, "Just by turning up and being there, you bring the presence of God."

I have brought this truth to mind many times since as I have gone to see people in desperate need. When thoughts pop into my head like "What's the point of you going?", "What on earth can you do?", or "They don't want to see you now", I turn to the great truths that God is with me, that I am a temple of the Holy Spirit, that I have one with me who can bind up the broken-hearted, and that God loves to minister to us through each other.

It's an incredible thing that our finite, physical bodies house the omnipresent and omnipotent creator of the universe. As I nervously peddle my bike along the road to someone's house, it's a sobering, and highly faith building thought, that as a Christian I am the very dwelling place of God. As I knock on the door, I trust that the hand of God is not invisible but has flesh and bones, first in the person of Jesus, and second in the body of his people—the church.

This world needs Spirit-filled, fired-up believers to go into every nation and proclaim the gospel with power, to sing in prison cells and miraculously walk out of jails, to lay their hands on the sick, and to raise the dead. If we have the Holy Spirit then we have what it takes to do what Jesus did, so let's be confident in giving away what we have.

QUESTIONS

1) Have you experienced times when the Holy Spirit has filled you or come upon you? Were you seeking it or expecting it in some way? What was it like?

2) What difference has being filled with the Spirit made to your life or what difference do you think it would make?

3) How can you seek to cultivate an ongoing awareness and enjoyment of God's loving power and presence in your life?

3. WIELD THE NAME

"in the name of
Jesus Christ of Nazareth"
Acts 3:6

FIXING BICYCLES

A friend came round to fix my bicycle recently. I knew that sooner or later I would have to sort it out again myself, so I watched what he did really closely, in order to learn. The fact that I had previously tried to fix it myself, and failed, helped focus my attention and prompted many questions. How were the brakes supposed to move? What did he undo to adjust them? "Ah, so that's how you do that!"

If you know you are going to do something a bit tricky, you watch and listen intently to any demonstration or instruction. This is the situation we are in right now as we "reach for fruit in supernatural healing". Jesus has said to his followers "Heal the sick" (Matthew 10:8), and we are looking at Peter and John doing just that.

We have seen some of Jesus' healing miracles, and now we are looking at the first recorded healing miracle of his disciples. This is really helpful as they are doing exactly what we have been commanded to do. Perhaps, like me, you have already given it a go and had mixed results. Well, that should cause us to look all the more intently at what Peter and John are doing right here.

So far, we have seen how they seized the moment. It was an ordinary, everyday situation, but they didn't just walk past: they had massive confidence that God was going to use them to do something supernatural. In the previous chapter we also saw the huge importance of the Holy Spirit. When Jesus ascended to be with his Father there was a dynamic pause—like a roller coaster stopping for a moment at the top of an incline before charging on and down the other side—then the Holy Spirit is poured out, the gun goes off, and the church is out of the starting blocks.

WHAT'S IN A NAME?

As well as the Spirit, the disciples have also been given a name, and this is what we will be looking at in this chapter. Names are really useful things, and they function in a number of interrelated ways.

First, a name helps us bring someone to mind. Think of those spider diagrams that are often used for brainstorming: they have a word in the middle of the page, and then lines coming out linking it to other related ideas. For example, you might have "my new car" in the middle with links to "fast", "green", and "expensive" around it. Sometimes those words might be connected to others producing a network of interconnected nodes.

When we think of a person's name, something similar fires up in our brains, and we are immediately aware of certain facts that we associate with them: what they look like, what they have done for us, how they make us feel, whether they are kind or mean, their likes and dislikes.

As we think more about them, our conscious mind moves about this web, experiencing who they are and what they mean to us. If we like them we might feel happy, but we might also begin to miss them if they are not around. We might suddenly remember that they asked us to pick up a pint of milk from the shops and decide to pop out after lunch. A name also helps us make plans that involve a particular person. We could consider inviting Bill, Bob, and Brenda to our party, for example.

In these ways, a name has a powerful impact on our mental and emotional world. As we think of the name of Jesus, therefore, our mind is impacted by who he is and what he has done for us. It's not just mind games and psychology though. The name of Jesus cannot be separated from the Spirit of Jesus. When we meditate on the name of Jesus, we can actually encounter Jesus by the Holy Spirit.

That brings us to the second way a name can function: as a means of getting hold of someone. It's hard to believe there was a time without mobile phones and Skype, but once upon a time some people used to talk to each other via citizens' band radios, or CBs as they were called. Since lots of people could be listening in, you needed to be clear about who you wanted to get hold of. This was done using their "handle", a unique name identifying them over the airwaves. It was so important that the first thing you asked a fellow CB user was "What's your handle, good buddy?" Once you had their name you could get hold of them again. In a similar way, all through the Bible, God reveals his names so that people can get hold of him. In doing so he makes himself knowable, accessible, and deployable. It's like he gives us his CB handle or his phone number and says, "Call me."

So a name affects our private, internal world and it lets us get in touch with someone, but there is a third way that a name can work. When some slight altercation arises between siblings, they might shout out "Mummy" or "Daddy". They know that these names will call in their parents. They are the means by which the power and influence of Mum and Dad are brought to bear in a given situation. Have you noticed the way children wield the words "I'm telling Mum / Dad / Teacher" with such devastating force? It's amazing how a name can make a person's presence felt, even before they are physically there.

The more powerful a person is and the more clearly defined their wishes, the greater effect their name will have. The use of someone's name carries with it their agenda as well as their ability to implement it. When a police officer calls out, "Stop in the name of the law!" they are not just expressing their own desire. Their use of the name frames the whole situation, not only in terms of the nation's laws, but also its means of enforcing them. It may just be one lone police officer calling out, but from that point on the presence and power of the law will be increasingly felt through helicopters, judges and prison officers.

In this way, a name can have a powerful impact even when the person is not physically present. The Bible implies that we can be present spiritually in a different place to our physical bodies (1 Corinthians 5:3–5; Colossians 2:5; Ephesians 2:6), and that is clearly the case with Jesus. He may not be physically present, but he has promised to be with us in the person of the Holy Spirit (Matthew 18:20), and as we speak in his name he turns up to further his agenda.

JESUS' AGENDA

I hope by now, after having spent several chapters in the first half of this book looking at the healing miracles of Jesus, that we have a pretty clear idea of what Jesus' agenda is. He touched a leper and made him well, healed a centurion's servant with a word, and at his touch, the fever left Peter's mother-in-law (Matthew 8:3, 8, 15). Jesus healed all the demon-possessed and sick who were brought to him, commanding a paralytic to get up and a dead girl to rise (Matthew 8:16; 9:1, 18). A lady who touched Jesus' garment was instantly made well, and two blind men got their sight back (Matthew 9:20, 29). There is no getting away from it, no watering it down, or ducking the issue: when

Jesus walked this earth he healed all who came to him. We can be sure, therefore, that it's on Jesus' agenda to make people well and that he has the ability to make that happen.

I remember a particular computer game that allowed you to target an enemy spaceship with a guided missile. Instead of wildly firing away at them and mostly missing, you carefully got one in your sights and then locked onto it. A little square appeared and followed the hapless alien around as your missile homed in on it and blew it to pieces. When we speak out in the name of Jesus, we mark out the situations we encounter with Jesus' plans. This situation or that sickness is now targeted with the name of Jesus. The Holy Spirit will make sure that Jesus' influence is felt and his plans are brought into being.

Even though Jesus is not physically present in the sense that we can press through the crowd and touch his garment, we do have his name, and with it we can take hold of him and make his influence felt. Through the name of Jesus, we can see God's power released and his presence experienced. As we speak out in the name of Jesus, the power of God in the person of the Holy Spirit is once again released into the world.

The religious authorities knew the connection between a name and a power. That's why they asked Peter and John, "By what power or by what name did you do this?" (Acts 4:7). They knew that real power comes from a person, not a plug socket. In our scientific age we usually think of power in terms of impersonal forces like gravity or electricity, but we must not think of God's power like this. Here, we are talking about personal power: the kind exerted by kings and rulers, visible and invisible. That sort of power comes with a plan, so once you know the name you know something of the agenda.

When Peter explains how the lame man was made well, he talks about a name:

> ... let it be known to all of you and to all the people of Israel that by the name of Jesus Christ of Nazareth,

whom you crucified, whom God raised from the dead-
by him this man is standing before you well. (Acts 4:10)

Did you get that? The words "by the *name* of Jesus" mean the
same as "by him". Jesus' power is exerted through the use of
his name.

TURN THE TAP ON

At the risk of undermining this personal aspect, perhaps a
picture is helpful at this point. In order to release a flow of
water from a tap, we need to grasp the handle and turn it. Now
think of the handle as Jesus' name. As we grasp hold of his
name and use it, power is released. Another term for this is
faith, which actively lays hold of the name of Jesus and releases
his power. Peter explains this to the excited crowd when he
says:

> It is by Jesus' name—by faith in his name—that this
> man was made strong ... The faith that is through Jesus
> has given the man this perfect health in the presence of
> you all. (Acts 3:16)

Peter and John simply took hold of the tap, turned the handle,
and released a flow of Holy Spirit power. It was never God's
intention that the Holy Spirit should be shut up in a reservoir,
but that he should stream out from the people of God as they
take hold of the mighty name of Jesus.

Before moving on there is an interesting turn of phrase that
stood out for me. Peter talks about "Faith that is through (or
by) Jesus" (Acts 3:16). Not just faith "in Jesus", or "by faith in
his name", but "faith that is through Jesus".

We find here the wonderful truth that this faith, this
decision to trust in and act on the powerful name of Jesus,
finds its origin in none other than the person of Jesus himself.
Jesus provokes people to faith in himself. He stimulates faith.

It's not simply that we stand here as impartial observers, sussing out Jesus. You may feel that is how it is, but it isn't. As Jesus is lifted up, he awakens and calls forth faith in men and women. His life, death, and resurrection are not only sufficient for our forgiveness and acceptance, but effective in drawing many to take hold of these things. He provides not only the means by which we are saved, that is his shed blood, but the disposition to appropriate it for ourselves through faith.

Reason can get us quite a long way. For example, we can hear testimonies of people being healed and think that God might do it again. There is, however, something special about faith that enables us to see and take hold of things that are beyond sight and reason (Hebrews 11:1). Faith enables us to see and do what the Father is doing. Faith enables us to see and take hold of the kingdom of heaven. Faith gives us X-ray vision to see through the natural foliage and reach out for the supernatural fruit that is there for the picking.

THE GLORY OF GOD'S NAME

So far we have seen how a name affects things, but there is also a sense in which a person can be affected by the way their name is used. I recently enjoyed singing along to some Messianic worship songs in Hebrew. Some of them are straight out of the Psalms, and I kept noticing that instead of singing the name of God (probably pronounced "Yahweh") they sing "Adoni", which means Lord. This is because the Jews took the third commandment "You shall not take the name of the LORD your God in vain" (Deuteronomy 5:11) so seriously that they didn't even speak God's name for fear of misusing it.

A reverence for God's name is entirely appropriate, but we have been given the name of Jesus to use. He wants us to use the name of Jesus in such a way as to bring him glory. We do so as we worship Jesus and declare what he has done, but also when we pray or speak out in the name of Jesus (John 14:13). God is determined to bring glory to himself through his son, so as we use the name of Jesus, especially in healing, we can have great confidence that God will gloriously back it up. He is jealous for his name (Ezekiel 39:25), and there is just no way that he is going to stand back and do nothing as we command healing in the name of his son.

ARMED AND DANGEROUS

Jesus came to destroy the works of the evil one: things like sin, sickness, and death—basically all the bad stuff. He did it decisively, by his death and resurrection. His very name "Jesus" means "God saves", and that is exactly who he is and what he did. We are given his name and, through it, the authority to wield his power and his victory over sin and death.

When you join the army you are given a gun. When you become a Christian you are given a name. It's like being handed a loaded rifle, so why not try pointing it at oppression and sickness, and squeezing off a few rounds?

At the risk of overdoing the gun metaphor, maybe the army rifle analogy doesn't do this justice. I remember playing a computer game when I was a student where you fought vicious man-eating dinosaurs. As you progressed through the levels, you picked up increasingly over-the-top weaponry until you got to the biggest one of all. As you pulled the trigger and held it down, the gun began to shake as the power levels built up. Arks of high-intensity plasma began crackling around the gun until the thing almost exploded in your hands. At that point you released the trigger and *wooosh!* A beam of high-energy radiation streamed into the oncoming T-Rex, totally obliterating it in a blinding flash of light. Back in the real world, the name of Jesus has that kind of power to destroy the works of darkness.

The rulers and authorities that opposed Peter and John knew this and commanded them not to "speak or teach at all in the name of Jesus" (Acts 4:18; 5:40). The name of Jesus is dangerous, and so they sought to disarm the disciples.

Spurgeon, the 19th century preacher, knew well the power of Jesus' name when he said:

> In the name Jesus, slumbers Omnipotence! The same power that made all the worlds lies hidden in that name! The power that will raise the dead and make new heavens and a new earth, is in that name, saving this poor fallen world from all its degradation, cleansing the planet of all the mists that now surround it, and bidding it shine forth like all its sister stars, to the glory of God who made it!! ... [The name of Jesus] has infinite power in it. (Spurgeon's Sermons: Volume 44, Number 2592, 1898)

AC/JC

Most of us are very familiar with AC power. It runs through our homes making our lights, TVs, and computers work. It is so important that without it much of modern civilisation would grind to a halt. More than AC power, though, the world desperately needs more JC power (I know that's a bit cheesy, but I couldn't resist it and it's true!). In fact, each Christian is meant to be part of an international grid delivering supernatural power into every city, town, and home. We do that as we step out in the name of Jesus Christ to heal and save and restore.

Ever since Genesis 4:26, God has been revealing his name, and people have been taking hold of it to release his power, not only to heal, but to save (Acts 2:21; 1 Corinthians 1:2). As Peter says:

> there is no other name under heaven given to men by which we must be saved. (Acts 4:12)

We absolutely must be saved from the terrible, corrosive, life-destroying effects of sin: I must, you must, everyone must. The consequences of not being saved are unthinkable, but God the Father has opened up a way. It is the only way, and it is through his beloved son Jesus. Having been forgiven through the name of Jesus, we know first-hand its power and potency, so let's wield it to full effect against sickness and disease.

QUESTIONS

1) If you had been with Peter and John after they had healed the lame beggar, what would you have asked them and why?

2) Write "Jesus" in the middle of a piece of paper, and then jot down around it all the words that come into your head when you think of Jesus. When you have done that, spend some time praying and worshipping Jesus for his amazing nature and qualities. Pray for people you know who are not well and ask, in Jesus' name, that they would be healed.

3) How can you glorify God more by the way you use the name of Jesus?

4. SAY THE WORD

"walk!"

Acts 3:6

WALKIES!

I once saw a small, four-year-old girl issuing commands to a large dog. In her cute, high-pitched voice she confidently and clearly told it to "Sit." The dog just stared back at her a bit bemused. Undeterred, she repeated the command again but louder and firmer this time: "Sit!" She didn't seem to question her right to give it orders. She clearly thought she wasn't doing anything wrong; it was the dog that was in the wrong—the dog needed to "get it". It was almost comical to watch. Until, that is, the dog suddenly sat down.

To understand why the dog sat, we need to see the bigger picture as there is more going on than meets the eye. The dog had been trained to respond to that command. Looking on, it shouldn't work; a little girl should not be able to order a big dog about, but she did.

In many ways, that is how it often looks and feels when you command healing in Jesus' name. When I command pain to go, or limbs to strengthen, or ears to hear, I feel a bit like a little girl telling a big dog to sit. It's laughable. Except that sometimes the pain goes, the limb is strengthened, and the ear opens. Why is that? It's because of the bigger picture of the life, death, and resurrection of Jesus Christ and the authority that we have in his name.

So far, as we have looked at the healing of the lame man, we have seen how Peter and John seized the moment ("Peter directed his gaze at him"); were confident that God would work through them (saying "Look at us"); and wielded the name of Jesus (commanding "In the name of Jesus Christ of Nazareth"). Let's now look at the next thing they say to the lame man. It's just one little word, but it's a wonderful one and packed with encouragement for us. Quite simply, they tell him to "walk!"

JESUS' AUTHORITY AND OUR AUTHORITY

The centurion, who said to Jesus "just say the word and my servant will be healed" (Matthew 8:8), saw the bigger picture. Jesus told paralysed men to "Get up ... and walk", and they did (John 5:8; Mark 2:9; Matthew 9:6). He told a man with a withered hand to stretch it out, and it was healed as he did so (Luke 6:10). Jesus even commanded the dead to come to life, ordering a young man to "get up" out of a coffin (Luke 7:14) and his dead friend Lazarus to "come out" of the grave (John 11:43). I don't know about you, but I find that level of authority totally awesome.

That is Jesus in action, but what about us? Well, here in our passage, Peter is doing the same thing—operating in the same authority and getting the same results. Peter says to the lame man, "In the name of Jesus Christ of Nazareth, rise up and walk" (Acts 3:6), and the man gets up and starts walking around. Jesus said that those who had faith in him would command mountains to move (Matthew 21:21), and at the beginning of Acts, Jesus' disciples get to work rearranging the geography.

Of course, we need to pray. James tells us to "pray for one another so that you may be healed" (James 5:16), and Paul prayed before healing an official's son:

> It happened that the father of Publius lay sick with fever and dysentery. And Paul visited him and prayed, and putting his hands on him healed him. (Acts 28:8)

But we also need to step into this dynamic of authority whereby we command things to line up with God's kingdom purposes. We need to remember that our prayers are not works by which we attempt to purchase healing from God. We are not heard because of our many words, nor is there any need to persuade God to heal. He already wants to. There is a time, therefore to stop praying to God and start speaking to bodies.

WORDS HAVE POWER

Words release power. God used them to bring the world into being. Jesus used them to still storms and heal people. We can wield them to grow legs, remove cancers, and open ears.

You may remember the playground rhyme: "Sticks and stones may break my bones, but words can never hurt me", and you have probably discovered that it isn't true. Words can hurt terribly. I prefer an alternative version of the rhyme that goes "Sticks and stones may break my bones, but words can heal them through faith in the name of Jesus!" Ok, it may not rhyme, but it is at least true! Words really can knit bones back together again.

I love the story I heard once of a sound technician at a huge gathering of people where the German evangelist Reinhard Bonnke was speaking. He reported hearing the crack of bones snapping back into place as healing was commanded in Jesus' name. Words can strengthen muscles that have not been used for decades. Words can cause cancerous cells to die and fall off. Words can cause lifelong pain to disappear. Words can open deaf ears and make blind eyes see.

"CLEAR OFF!"

I was once walking past a toddlers' playground with someone. Some teenagers were sitting on the top of the slide, obviously ignoring a big sign forbidding older children from using it. I thought to myself, "Oh, that's a shame; I hope they don't damage it too much. Still, never mind, it happens a lot, and what can you do?"

As I was thinking this, I realised my companion was walking over to the group. Words were exchanged, presumably to establish that they were not just "big kids". Then, amazingly, they got down and walked away. Now, I reckon that one of the reasons he felt so confident doing that was because he was a school teacher and was used to exercising authority over young people. He does it every day, so when he sees something that is not right rather than shrug his shoulders and walk on, he sorts it out with his words.

My point, of course, is not about looking after age-appropriate play equipment but that we have this attitude to sickness. It shouldn't be there, and we can do something about it. We need to carry in our spirit a sense of our authority and confidently command illness to clear off!

Peter commanded the man to "rise up", and he actually obeyed. The command effectively extended the kingdom of God so that it broke out in this man's body. They weren't saying, "Get up, you fraud, we know you can walk" or helping him get over some psychological block in using his legs. A person like you and me was commanding a man to get up who had been physically unable to walk for his whole life (remember this man had to be carried everywhere) and, what's more, he did. He got up!

I thank God for the answers to prayer that I have seen. On many occasions we have prayed for pain to go from backs, joints, or heads, and it has! Sometimes the pain had been there for months and had been very debilitating, but when we prayed in the name of Jesus it went, either immediately or a short time afterwards. I remember briefly praying with a friend for someone with tinnitus after which he said it was 70% better. These healings can make a massive difference to people's lives, and I am grateful for every single one, but I never want to dial down the amazing quality of the healing miracles in the Bible.

Even as I see things begin to happen around me, they are often of a different order of magnitude to the ones recorded in the book of Acts. I praise God when pain leaves a person's knee or a headache gets 90% better, but Jesus has promised even greater things. I long to see the name of Jesus regularly triumph over multiple sclerosis, release people from lifelong paralysis, and destroy terminal cancer.

THE GOSPEL

The gospel itself is not just a proclamation; it comes with a command. The good news of what God has done in Christ is followed with the imperative to "Repent and believe" (Mark 1:15). The gospel, along with this command, extends the kingdom of God into the hearts and minds of men and women. It's not a suggestion or recommendation or even simply an invitation. It's a verbal command. Rather like "Rise up and walk."

In the very passage we are looking at, just after telling people who Jesus is and what he has done, Peter says, "Repent, therefore, and turn again, that your sins may be blotted out" (Acts 3:19). Jesus also commanded repentance and faith when he:

> went into Galilee, proclaiming the good news of God and saying, "The time is fulfilled, and the kingdom of God is at hand; repent and believe in the gospel." (Mark 1:15)

His disciples did the same thing when "they went out and proclaimed that people should repent" (Mark 6:12), and they continued to do this after the outpouring of the Spirit:

> Peter said to them, "Repent and be baptized every one of you in the name of Jesus Christ for the forgiveness of your sins, and you will receive the gift of the Holy Spirit." (Acts 2:38)

Paul explains to King Agrippa that he "preached that [people] should repent and turn to God" (Acts 26:20), and he tells the men of Athens that God "commands all people everywhere to repent" (Acts 17:30). Finally, John writes to the church:

> This is [God's] commandment, that we believe in the name of his Son Jesus Christ and love one another, just as he has commanded us. (1 John 3:23)

Some people like exercising authority but have to be careful to do so with people's best interest at heart. Others are not so comfortable exerting themselves in this way but need to grow stronger in it for the benefit of others. There is no getting away from it though, whether it is through the gospel message or healing the sick, a disciple of Jesus is to walk in and wield massive authority. If we don't, we are like a coal miner tickling the rock face with the end of his pickaxe. Conversely, each time we exert our authority, the pick strikes the rock, sparks fly, cracks appear, and chunks break off.

LEND A HAND

In the Old Testament, the law did not come with the power to obey it. Of course, the problem was not with the commands, which were good, but with us, who are not. However, in the New Covenant things are very different. The gospel comes with the resurrection power of Jesus to live free. In the same way, when Peter told the man to get up, his command was accompanied by a release of power enabling the man to actually obey.

I love the way Peter extends his hand to help the man up. "He took him by the right hand and raised him up" (Acts 3:7). There is a ton of truth right there in these few words. First, they remind us again of the power of physical touch: when a Spirit-filled believer touches someone in need, heaven's potential can be earthed.

Second, there is the relational dynamic: Peter's extended hand speaks of personal connection and identification. Kingdom advance rarely happens at arm's length, and Peter is not about to stand by and watch this man struggle to his feet on his own, so he steps forward and helps him up. Think of the way a midwife helps deliver a baby. She gets involved and helps draw out the precious new life with her words and actions, and so it seems to me that Peter is helping to bring this precious miracle to birth. He not only says "Rise up" but helps the man to get up, and all the while God is helping the man up through Peter.

It's the same with the gospel. When we exhort people to trust in Jesus for the forgiveness of their sins, there are all sorts of ways we can help them, but ultimately the enabling power comes from God.

Proclaiming the gospel is ultimately an act of authority, and God uses the command to bring people to new life in him. Now, that doesn't mean it's not proclaimed politely, with respect, gentleness, and humility. Authority doesn't increase with volume or rudeness, and it isn't to be equated with shouting or being pushy. Sometimes these things can actually betray a lack of authority—or at least some insecurity or lack of confidence in handling it.

SATAN THROWN DOWN
We are designed and destined to exercise authority. When God made the first man, he commanded him to rule over the earth.

Sadly, Adam rebelled, and we have inherited his deadly tendency. Each of us has got our hands caught in the till in one form or another and have been given the sack. Through Jesus' death and resurrection, however, we are taken on again and restored to rule. Let's explore this important truth a little more by looking first at Luke 10 and then at Ephesians 2.

In Luke 10:18–19 we see that Jesus sent seventy-two disciples out to heal, deliver, and proclaim the kingdom of God. When they came back, they were ecstatic: "People are getting healed; this is awesome" they said (my paraphrase). Jesus then counsels them not to rejoice primarily in their kingdom accomplishments, but in their personal salvation. That remains sound advice for those of us seeking to move in the supernatural, but listen to what Jesus says next:

> I saw Satan fall like lightning from heaven...Behold, I have given you authority to tread on serpents and scorpions, and over all the power of the enemy, and nothing shall hurt you. (Luke 10:18–19)

At first I thought this was saying that Satan had come down to cause mischief and that Jesus had sent the disciples to stop him, but that only skims the surface of what Jesus is really saying and misses the heart of it. Satan is pictured here as falling. He is passive in it, like someone who falls down the stairs. Imagine the steps on the stage of a popular TV talent show. This verse is not saying that Satan steps down them in a controlled, powerful, majestic sort of way, wind blowing in his hair, while powerful upbeat music plays. The truth is he trips and lands in a crumpled heap at the bottom. It's like he slips on a banana skin with all the subsequent and sudden loss of poise and control.

Other scriptures support the sense of Satan being pushed or thrown down. When you throw something, down it moves faster than it would under gravity alone. There is a hidden force behind the speed of his fall as he is booted out of heaven (Isaiah 14:12; Revelation 12:9).

Heaven is a place of authority because God dwells there, and his throne is the ultimate seat of all power. While Satan's expulsion does not mean that he is no longer dangerous (1 Peter 5:8; Revelation 12:12), we must not let go of the fact that he is a fallen, disgraced, and prone foe.

Come with me, if you will, to an English country estate where a gamekeeper is hunting grouse. He is tracking a bird in flight through the sights of his double-barrelled shotgun. Sitting at his side is his trusty hound. The gamekeeper squeezes the trigger. Bang! It's a bullseye and the grouse falls like a stone to the ground. He looks down at the dog and issues the command: "Fetch."

The dog goes haring off into the fields to find its prey. It could never have got the bird while it was in the air, but now it's been ignominiously brought down it's a different story. Generations of breeding and years of training allow it to home in on its target.

Now that, I think, is like the picture Jesus is painting to his disciples. Satan has been shot down, and Jesus is commanding his disciples to "Fetch." In fact, you could say that the great commission, foreshadowed in the sending out of the seventy-two, is essentially Jesus looking at his disciples, and us, and saying "Fetch!"

Pinpointing the time that Jesus is referring to is tricky as it is increasingly applicable in a number of places in history. First, there is Satan's initial rebellion (Isaiah 14:12 may be referring to this); second, his defeat by Jesus on the cross (Colossians 2:5); and finally, his future fate of being thrown into the lake of burning sulphur (Revelation 20:10). It seems, therefore, that Jesus is making a statement that has increasing and unfolding validity throughout history. The fact that we cannot pinpoint a time is not actually that much of a problem since the application is clear. No matter how much he puffs himself up, no matter what he does and how things look, Satan is a defeated foe, fighting a losing battle, and is vulnerable to those sent out in Jesus' authority.

We must not, therefore, let past experience or current challenges deceive us into the delusion of impotence. We have been given power and authority—so let's use it. In the Garden of Eden, the first hint of the gospel was revealed in the promise that the woman's seed would crush the serpent's head (Genesis 3:15). Jesus himself fulfils that, but we, in Christ, are involved in the mop-up operation—the great "fetch" of faith.

WE ARE LIFTED UP

It's so important that we get this, and it's so counter-intuitive to my experience that I want to look at our authority again from another perspective. You may be familiar with the fact that Jesus is seated enthroned in heaven with all power and authority. God the Father:

> raised him from the dead and seated him at his right hand in the heavenly places, far above all rule and authority and power and dominion, and above every name that is named, not only in this age but also in the one to come. And he put all things under his feet and gave him as head over all things to the church. (Ephesians 1:20–22)

What may come as more of a surprise, is that we are there with him. It's not just that Satan has been thrown down but that we have been lifted up. You see, in Ephesians, Paul goes on to say:

> [God] made us alive together with Christ—by grace you have been saved—and raised us up with him and seated us with him in the heavenly places in Christ Jesus. (Ephesians 2:5–6)

If you are a Christian, you are seated with Christ in heavenly places, and that's not just for the view! It's to exercise authority, and the main way we do that is with our words.

HIRING AND FIRING

In Acts chapter 3, Peter is exercising his authority over a fallen foe as one who is enthroned with Christ in heavenly places. He looks at this man who has never used his legs and says, "Get up and walk." We need to open our mouths and speak with authority to bring in the kingdom of God. Even in the apparently natural realm, authority is often very effectively exercised through words. When you tell your dog to sit, it should sit. If it doesn't, it does not lessen your authority or cause you to say, "Oh, perhaps I don't have authority over my dog." You do have authority, and you should keep exerting it. When you tell your children to brush their teeth, they should do it. Whether they do it or not, does not affect the legitimacy of your authority as a parent.

Now, there is of course a process involved in exercising authority. There are battles that have to be fought and discussions that need to be had, but we must not give up. Sometimes parents have needed to put their children to bed one hundred times before they stay put. The next night it may take less. And the next even less. In the end, a few words usually do the trick. We are in a battle, and we need to keep pushing forward to establish a culture of healing.

In the popular TV program "The Apprentice", when Sir Alan Sugar points his finger at a would-be apprentice and says, "You're fired", they are fired. They can try to stay around and carry on in the competition, but it will get increasingly hard for them as everyone knows they've been fired. The cameras won't film them, and they will not be included in the next challenges and will simply be told, "You're fired, go home." We need to get used to telling sickness, oppression, depression, and injustice—"You're fired!"

At the end of the series, of course, Sir Alan says to someone "You're hired." We don't just fire things in the Spirit; we also hire them. In fact, in Acts 3, Peter is speaking positively to the man rather than negatively to his sickness. God wants us to have confidence in his authority and command the blind to see, the deaf to hear, and the lame to walk. As we do so, we are crushing scorpions and serpents. In this world there is no shortage of sickness, injustice, addiction, and oppression. If you are a Christian, Jesus has given you authority, so why not get stomping!

QUESTIONS

1) Do you command healing as well as pray for it? Think about how you could, sensitively but authoritatively, command healing more when you are praying for someone who is not well. What would you say?

2) How do you feel when you command healing in Jesus' name? What thoughts come into your head? To what extent do they line up with reality? How can you overcome any negative thoughts or feelings and speak out healing in Jesus' name?

3) In commanding healing, how does it help you to know that Satan has been shot down and that you are seated in heavenly places?

5. GIVE THE EXPLANATION

"Why does this surprise you?"
Acts 3:12

NEW YEAR'S RESOLUTIONS

As I come to consider the next aspect of this healing miracle, it is the beginning of January, a time when many people make New Year's resolutions. They resolve to spend more time with family, get fit, quit smoking, or just enjoy life more. Not everyone enters the New Year with such optimism though. I heard one guy remark that making New Year's resolutions almost guarantees that they will fail.

It seems to me that much of the cynicism about resolutions is due to a failure to distinguish between two sorts. The first sort are all about us. We say, "I, out of my own resources and determination, am going to do such and such." You may have grown disillusioned with that sort because they rely on your own abilities. They are fundamentally about us trying harder and usually have their origin in our own hearts and minds. They can be rather self-centred too. Little wonder then that they usually fail, but don't get them mixed up with the second sort of resolution.

The second sort are all about God. They have their origin in God, in who he is, what he wants, and what he can do. This kind of resolution is an entirely different strain all together. They are superalloys forged from the scriptures we have been looking at, along with other verses such as John 13:34, Mark 16:15–18, Acts 1:8, and John 14:14. In case you are wondering, a superalloy mixes two metals to get the best properties of both. They tend to be used in high-performance contexts, such as jet engines—and following Jesus!

The first sort of resolution is about our ability, whereas the second sort is about God's grace. Another name for the second sort is "faith" because they are effectively a decision to believe in, and act in line with, who God is and what he has said. If you are going to make resolutions, base them on what God has done in Christ and all that he has promised to do through Him.

Why not make resolutions based on the fact that God can and will heal people, physically and supernaturally? Base them on all you see in Matthew 8 and 9, and Acts 3 and 4. Base them on God, as revealed in the person of Jesus, who went around healing people and commissions his disciples to be agents and ministers of healing today.

SALVATION SIGNS

It seems to me that the more important a place is, the more crucial it is to have lots of clear signs to direct people there. Most cities I have visited are liberally sprinkled with signs to their hospital's accident and emergency department (A&E). Even if we know how to get there, it would be rather antisocial to cover them up for other people who don't. Yet when we neglect healing as a key part of the great commission, we effectively do just that.

I have been deliberately focusing on physical healing, not just because it is a key element of the passages we have been looking at, but because healing is often spiritualised far too quickly. It is true that a blind man receiving his sight points to the truth that Jesus can enable us to see spiritually with our hearts. The trouble is that glossing over the reality of the physical healing undermines both the effectiveness of the sign and the reality that it points to. If Jesus didn't really heal people, does he really save people? God wants people to be well in body and spirit. That's why he heals them. The demonstration of this fact in physical terms points to the greater and deeper healing available through God's forgiveness of our sin and adoption as sons and daughters.

When our children had parties, we would hang a bunch of balloons on the front door to show the guests that they had come to the right house. Now balloons are not some arbitrary symbol of a party; they are an indispensable part of the party itself. You can't have a party without balloons! In the same way, a healing is not simply just a sign of God's kingdom but an integral part of the kingdom itself. When people get healed, the kingdom of heaven is breaking out right there and then, not in some other part of town in a completely different way. Supernatural healings are the multicoloured party balloons pinned to the door of the kingdom of heaven.

In Acts 3, a man totally lame from birth jumps up to his feet. This is the key event in the passage upon which everything else hinges. It's not a side issue. It's essential that we get it and understand it: God heals. It is really important that we know that the name of Jesus is powerful over sickness and death— that God really does use ordinary men and women like you and me to cure cancer and restore sight.

If you are a Christian you really do have that kind of authority. You can say, "Get up!" and have a lame man get up. Any lack of healing in our experience must not be allowed to corrode the steel framework of God's word; rather, it should galvanise us into action. There are simply not enough salvation signs in our cities.

Having said all that, and amazing though this healing is, it is not the end of the story. The best is yet to come. The main point of the healing is about to be revealed. Only a small fraction of the words in Acts 3 and 4 are about the man being healed; the rest fill out the reason for it. It's like the classic iceberg analogy where only 10% is visible above the water line. It is the ice beneath the water that has the ship-sinking momentum, and it is the same here. Of course the beggar is healed because God is loving and kind and wants people to be well, but his goodness and kindness can have a far more life changing effect than just this man's physical wellbeing.

Let's read on in Acts chapter 3 and into chapter 4 to see where this supernatural sign leads. As we go below the waterline, three things come into view:

1. HEALING GETS OUR ATTENTION

First, supernatural healing gets our attention. When the lame man entered the temple leaping and praising God, everyone noticed him. There were lots of people milling around, just like your local shopping mall on Christmas Eve, but this man stood out. He was shouting out his testimony, but his actions spoke even louder than his words:

> ... all the people saw him walking and praising God, and recognized him as the one who sat at the Beautiful Gate of the temple, asking for alms. (Acts 3:9–10)

Everyone noticed. Healing is like a foghorn sounding in the busyness of life. There is so much going on, so much to think about: work, family, relationships, kids, house, hopes, and fears, then *honnnnk!* "Wow, that guy got healed!" Just like the emergency services have flashing lights to distinguish them from all the other lights on the road, healing is God's way of getting our attention on the highway of life. It's like a tray dropping in a cafeteria. Crash! Everyone looks. It's not just that it is loud, but rather that the sound is qualitatively different.

The clash of cutlery rings out over the drone of a hundred hungry voices.

When someone gets healed it focuses our attention. God is just as much behind science as he is behind the supernatural. He can make the sun move in the sky, and he can make it stand still (Joshua 10:13). In fact, you need the natural to notice the *supe*rnatural. The natural and the supernatural works of God are like the dot and dash of Morse code. It's the difference that enables information to be conveyed.

Whenever a message arrives on my phone, it beeps or it buzzes in my pocket. Either way, it interrupts my current train of thought to let me know that someone wants to communicate with me. Each healing miracle is a beep or buzz from God to let us know he wants to tell us something; he wants us to know he is a healer and a saviour.

2. HEALING GETS US THINKING

Second, miraculous healing gets us thinking. Acts 3:10 goes on:

> They were filled with wonder and amazement at what had happened to him. (Acts 3:10; cf. Luke 4:36; 5:9)

The words "wonder" and "amazement" span a massive range of meanings from fear to delight. Healing stirs up our emotions and our minds. It throws everything up into the air and causes us to wonder and to process what we are seeing and hearing. We think again and re-evaluate the world in which we live.

Each of us has a set of more or less well-ordered beliefs about the world and the way it works that make up our world view. When someone gets miraculously healed, our beliefs can get thrown up into the air like a pack of cards. In fact, the Greek word translated "amazed" can mean "throwing the mind out of its normal state." Once we have picked up all our thoughts again, we may find they are arranged in a brand new order.

Many of us can live for a long time with a world view that behaves like a stubborn mule, refusing to budge an inch. Supernatural healing walks up behind that mule and gives it a great big *slap* on its rear end. We might think that matter and energy are all that there is, just blind impersonal forces moving things about, and that everything is described or even determined by mathematical equations. Many people believe that we appear, go through life, and then just wink out of existence. We can think there is no God (or gods) and that science is the only true gatekeeper of truth. But when we, or someone we know, gets supernaturally healed from lifelong paralysis, our world view gets a wallop and lurches forward.

Others might believe that while there may be more to life than meets the eye, we can't really know for sure. When someone gets healed of blindness, or a cancer literally falls off, *whack*, that world view often clears off too.

For some though, the spiritual side of life is all too real. They know they are under the oppressive control of a power greater than themselves. They live in fear and bondage, or paralysing, hopeless regret for things they have seen, done, or had done to them. Their unmovable mule is that there is no hope. Then a deaf man hears, or a blind man sees, and *smack!* Hope comes that there is a higher power at work in the world that is far greater than the one enslaving them.

Have you ever woken up and discovered that the whole country has come to a standstill because of a heavy snowfall? All your plans for the day need rethinking. There is a new reality to be confronted and worked out. A white canvas with new challenges and new possibilities is stretched out before you. Life becomes a whole new ballgame of sledging, snowballs, and snowmen. It's the same when someone gets supernaturally healed. It changes everything.

3. HEALING DEMANDS AN EXPLANATION

So when someone gets healed, it gets our attention, and it gets us thinking. Read through Acts, and you will see that this happened time and time again in the early church:

> The crowds with one accord paid attention to what was being said by Philip when they heard him and saw the signs that he did. For ... many who were paralyzed or lame were healed. So there was much joy in that city. (Acts 8:6–8)

They paid attention to what was being said, but what exactly was being said? Once God has got people's attention, what does he want to say? Once he has broken through the static buzz of information overload, or snapped us out of our petty preoccupations, what does he want to communicate?

Peter uses the healing to preach one of the richest gospel messages found in the whole Bible. He tells people exactly who Jesus is, what he has done, and how it fits in with the whole of salvation history. This healing becomes a window into the past and the future with some pressing decisions to be made in the present.

Just like in Acts 2, Peter's sermon in Acts 3 is essentially an explanation of supernatural phenomena (Acts 2:14; 3:12, 16). With this man walking beside him, Peter tells everyone how "by faith in the name of Jesus ... was this man made strong" (Acts 3:16). This same Jesus, who they just crucified, is very much alive and well and, through faith, bringing life and health to others. "Repent therefore", he goes on, "and turn [to God] that your sins may be blotted out" (Acts 3:19).

A paraphrase of his argument might go something like this: "Hey, this man just got healed in the name of Jesus. In this same name you can also find forgiveness, know God's love, and inherit eternal life. Find those things hard to accept? Well, excuse me, but a man born lame is now leaping around over there. That's also hard to accept, but it's true nonetheless."

Peter does it again in chapter 4 when they are being questioned by the religious authorities. He uses the healing as the context to preach the gospel:

> If you ask by what means this man was healed, … let it be known to all of you and to all the people of Israel that by the name of Jesus Christ of Nazareth, whom you crucified, whom God raised from the dead—by him this man is standing before you, well..... and there is salvation in no one else, for there is no other name under heaven given among men by which we must be saved. (Acts 4:9–12)

In effect he says: "We know this will have caused you to think again. Your mind will be filled with some very pressing questions right now. Well, this Jesus, whom you put to death, is alive and well and healing people. He is the Messiah, the Saviour of the world. What do you make of that?"

Supernatural healing gives the gospel the existential high ground in the battle for human hearts. If I say, "Because of what Jesus did you can be forgiven and accepted by God", you might respond, "That's just a fairy tale", or "There is no God, and even if there was I would not be accountable to him." But when someone blind or lame from birth gets healed in front of you, I would guess those statements suddenly seem rather less forceful. In fact, those who opposed the disciples were silenced:

> Seeing the man who was healed standing beside them, they had nothing to say in opposition. (Acts 4:14)

Discussing their dilemma among themselves they ask:

> What shall we do with these men? For that a notable

sign has been performed through them is evident to all
the inhabitants of Jerusalem, and we cannot deny it.
(Acts 4:16)

It's hard to argue when there is a living testimony to God's love
and power standing in front of you. Healing is a very fruitful
context for the gospel, and in this case many people responded
and got saved. We read that the number of Christians "grew to
about five thousand" (Acts 4:4), and since it was probably only
men who were being counted, we could reasonably double that
estimate. Since the last figure we are given is three thousand, it
is likely that many hundreds believed on the back of this one
miracle alone.

This happens again and again. Take a look at what
happened when Philip preached the gospel to the Samaritans
with various miraculous signs:

> And the crowds with one accord paid attention to what
> was being said by Philip when they heard him and saw
> the signs that he did. For... many who were paralyzed or
> lame were healed. (Acts 8:4–8)

We know a great many believed in Jesus because it is recorded
that "Samaria accepted the word of God" (Acts 8:14). Then, on
the very next page in my Bible, I read that many were saved
when Peter healed Aeneas:

> Now as Peter went here and there among them all, he
> came down also to the saints who lived at Lydda. There
> he found a man named Aeneas, bedridden for eight
> years, who was paralyzed. And Peter said to him,
> "Aeneas, Jesus Christ heals you; rise and make your
> bed." And immediately he rose. And all the residents of
> Lydda and Sharon saw him, and they turned to the
> Lord. (Acts 9:32–35)

SHOW-AND-TELL

When we looked at the life of Jesus, we saw that healing was God's hallmark of authenticity. His plan and desire is that it should still be stamped on the good news that through Jesus' death and resurrection, forgiveness and acceptance are available to all.

In this chapter, we have seen that God still wants his gospel signposted with the supernatural, especially miracles of healing. We have also noted that healing is not only a sign but an integral part of the destination. Like the smell of freshly baked bread, healing is the anticipating aroma of the kingdom of God's future fullness.

When someone gets healed, the kingdom of God becomes visible and tangible. There is an objective phenomenon to be understood. It's like show-and-tell at school where children bring in something from home that they really love. They proudly display it to the class and are asked questions about it. Well, supernatural healing is something we can bring from our Father's throne room to show our friends. It helps us talk about and explain the fuller wonders and glory of his coming kingdom.

The sceptical anti-supernatural stance of so many can be a challenge at times, but it also presents us with an opportunity. In our modern world, where the natural workings of the universe are more clearly understood than they have ever been, the truly supernatural has the potential to stand out all the more. There is no doubt about it that now, more than ever, if we reach for fruit in supernatural healing, we will have a lot of explaining to do!

QUESTIONS

1) What resolutions do you want to make that will result in the extension of God's kingdom? Perhaps you could resolve to pray for more people to be healed or to keep praying until a particular person is made well.

2) How has seeing God work supernaturally affected your world view, or how would it? What "stubborn mules" would get a whack?

3) Have you ever had the opportunity to explain the gospel on the back of a healing miracle? What did you, or would you, say to explain it to someone who knew little or nothing of the gospel?

6. PRESS THROUGH
IN PRAYER

"they lifted their voices together to God"
Acts 4:24

FACING FIERCE OPPOSITION

We have looked in some detail now not only at a number of Jesus' healing miracles but also at the first recorded healing miracle of his disciples. It is my hope and prayer that your faith has risen, your expectation has increased, and that your resolve to reach for the supernatural has begun to produce fruit.

There is one more thing, though, that we need to draw out of this passage before we finish. In order to give a full and faithful picture of what happens when the gospel is preached in the context of supernatural healing, we need to look a little bit closer at Acts chapter 4. If we don't, we may get a nasty surprise later on. While miracles can help many come to faith, the truth is that not everyone is won over by wonders, and this was certainly the case in the first century.

As the number of miracles increased, we read:

> ... they were all together in Solomon's Portico. None of
> the rest dared join them, but the people held them in

high esteem. And more than ever believers were added
to the Lord. (Acts 5:12–16)

So, two things are going on here. Yes, many people were drawn
in and came to faith, but others backed off and kept their
distance. People sometimes literally run away from miracles,
cursing and swearing. It shakes our world view when
something "impossible" happens and raises many
uncomfortable questions, so we run and hide in the lie of an
impersonal, amoral, pointless universe. But there is a third
reaction we need to be aware of. In the face of miracles, there
are some who are hardened into fierce opposition.

Though the Sadducees must have known that the healing
was genuine, it did not lead them to believe in Jesus. They did
not hold up their hands and say: "Oh no, we have made a
terrible mistake. Jesus is our Messiah, our Saviour. We believe!"
At first it's hard to relate to their reaction, and we just think of
them as evil, bad guys, but their motives are actually not too
dissimilar to the thoughts and issues that can swirl around in
our hearts today when we hear about Jesus.

First of all, in working hard at studying and keeping God's
commandments, they had begun to think they had done
enough; that they had met the required standard. Rather than
realising their total dependence on God's grace—his
forgiveness and gift of righteousness—they had become self-
righteous. What need had they then of Jesus, the Lamb of God
(John 1:29)? How ironic that the people responsible for the
temple and its sacrifices failed to recognise the one who was *the
temple* and *the sacrifice*.

Today we can still dishonour God's perfect goodness by
considering ourselves "good enough". Even after becoming a
Christian, you are not immune from this deception. As we
follow Jesus and our lives get increasingly cleaned up, we can
actually begin to be impressed with our progress and lose sight
of the fact that we are still a million miles away from God's

glorious moral perfection. We should, therefore, never stop trusting and rejoicing in Jesus' life, death, and resurrection as the means by which we are loved and accepted by God.

Secondly, the Sadducees liked to be the ones who taught people about God and so did not take kindly to being instructed by "common, uneducated" men (Acts 4:13). They loved being the source of truth but were too proud to learn about the one who is *the truth* (John 14:16). Today, with all our knowledge of science and history, we can think we know it all and fail to look carefully at the life and claims of Jesus.

Thirdly, like many today, the Sadducees did not believe in the resurrection of the dead (Matthew 22:23) and so were heavily invested in this life. No wonder they had difficulty with the one who was *the resurrection* (John 11:25).

Fourthly, being somewhere near the top of the social and economic strata of the times, they must also have struggled with Jesus' teaching about laying down your life to find it (Matthew 10:39; 16:25). They simply had too much to lose. As Jesus said, it is hard for a rich man to enter the kingdom of heaven (Matthew 19:24). It is such a tragedy that some can look at their life and what they have, and decide not to swap it for *the life* (John 14:6) and *the treasure* (Matthew 13:44) that is on offer in the person of Jesus.

A final and probably overriding reason why the Sadducees opposed the message about Jesus was that they wanted to remain in charge. They liked being in charge of their lives and the lives of others far too much to bow the knee to *the Lord of Lords* (Revelation 19:16). Again, that can be a real issue for us today as we hear about Jesus. We like being our own boss and calling the shots. Mercifully, God's love can, and does, break in. As we begin to realise how much of a mess we have made of our lives and how much Jesus has done for us, we gladly hand over the reins of our lives to him.

Sadly though, that is not always the case. Confronted with a clear healing miracle, the Sadducees, along with other powerful and influential men, were hardened in their unbelief and resolved to oppose the message and the messengers by all means possible.

THE FEAR FACTOR

The rulers and authorities seized Peter and John and put them in prison overnight to marinate in fear (Acts 4:3). Prisons tended to do that to you in those days. They were hard, dark, fearful places where people waited for some terrible punishment. When morning came, the religious leaders brought the disciples out and set them in their midst.

So that we don't miss the intensity of the intimidation, Luke tells us which faces glared down at them that day. It was the exact same group who got Jesus crucified (John 18:13, 24), led once more by Annas and Caiaphas (Acts 4:5–6). If you think you have been in some tight spots, or faced powerful intimidation, imagine how they must have felt.

The religious leaders' message was clear: "If you carry on speaking about Jesus and healing people in his name, we will make sure your death is slow, public, and painful. Remember what we did to Jesus?" Luke records that:

> they called them and charged them not to speak or teach at all in the name of Jesus. (Acts 4:18)

What can we learn from this? If you preach a powerless message that challenges and changes no one, few people will bother to oppose you. They may pity you, but it's unlikely they will ever exert themselves to persecute you. However, when people start getting healed in the name of Jesus, the stakes are raised and the knives come out. Very quickly, in the story of the early church, blood is shed and lives are lost. Soon after this event, Peter and John are once more arrested, and this time they are beaten. A little later, Stephen, another disciple, is seized and stoned to death (Acts 7:58). Before we reach for fruit in supernatural healing we would be wise, therefore, to count the cost.

SOVEREIGN LORD

If we are serious about stepping out in the supernatural, it seems opposition is certain. It may come in many forms and in many ways (imprisonment, intimidation, false accusations, increased temptation, or just feeling really stupid and silly), but it will come. When Peter and John released the power of Jesus into the life of a lame man, they saw thousands respond to the gospel, but they also experienced a vicious backlash. So how should we respond when we face such determined opposition?

When I was writing this final chapter, I attended a prayer meeting with some church leaders from around my city. I was so encouraged when "coincidentally" it was kicked off with the final part of Acts 3 and 4. It will be helpful for us to look at it and see how the disciples responded in the face of such fearful threats:

> And when they heard it, they lifted their voices together to God and said, "Sovereign Lord, who made the heaven and the earth and the sea and everything in them, who through the mouth of our father David, your servant, said by the Holy Spirit, " 'Why did the Gentiles rage, and the peoples plot in vain? The kings of the earth set themselves, and the rulers were gathered together, against the Lord and against his Anointed'— for truly in this city there were gathered together against your holy servant Jesus, whom you anointed, both Herod and Pontius Pilate, along with the Gentiles and the peoples of Israel, to do whatever your hand and your plan had predestined to take place. And now, Lord, look upon their threats and grant to your servants to continue to speak your word with all boldness, while you stretch out your hand to heal, and signs and wonders are performed through the name of

your holy servant Jesus." And when they had prayed, the place in which they were gathered together was shaken, and they were all filled with the Holy Spirit and continued to speak the word of God with boldness. (Acts 4:24–31)

What did Peter and John do? Well, first they prayed, but note the nature of the God they prayed to. It seems significant to me that, when faced with overwhelming difficulty and hardship, their prayers were saturated with the sovereignty of God. The majority of this prayer describes a God who is indisputably in charge of all the events of history. We are in the realm of mystery here, so don't think of God as controlling people like puppets, with no wills or responsibility of their own. People do what they will, but God works through them to bring about what he wills. You can try to oppose God as hard as you like only to find out that he has worked and weaved his unstoppable purposes through all that has taken place, both the good and the bad.

Analogies of God's sovereignty need to be handled carefully, but this dynamic reminds me of a particular self-defence technique. As your attacker runs towards you, fully committed to doing you harm, you grab their arms, stick your foot in their stomach, and roll backwards. As their body arcs over you, you help them on their way by straightening out your leg. The effectiveness of the move, and many others like it, is that all the malevolent force of your attacker is redirected towards their defeat. If you get it right, they end up on their back, several feet away from you, gasping for breath. This is what happened on the cross. Satan sought to destroy Jesus by getting him crucified, but it was precisely through Jesus' death on the cross that Satan himself was crushed and defeated.

Judas decided to betray Jesus and was morally responsible for it (Matthew 26:24). The Jews and the Romans crucified Jesus and were responsible for it (Luke 23:34; Acts 3:15). God, however, superintended these things to further his great plans and purposes (Isaiah 53:10). Was Judas right to betray Jesus? No. Was Pilate right to wash his hands of Jesus? No. Were the Roman soldiers doing a good thing when they whipped Jesus and hammered the nails into his hands and feet? No. But did God determine that these things should happen? Yes. Was God working through it all to save us from our sins and bring us into an eternal relationship with him? Yes. While people were intent on doing evil, God was intent on working it all for good, for "the saving of many lives" (Genesis 50:20).

We need the truth of God's sovereignty in our hearts as we extend the kingdom in all its aspects, especially in the area of physical healing. God wants people to be well, so we pray expecting people to get well, but no matter what the outcome, we can remain confident that he will work through all things for our good and his glory (Romans 8:28). If someone isn't healed, should we infer that it is God's will for them to be sick? No, no more than the resistance of poverty and injustice to the extension of God's kingdom persuades us that God is indifferent to these things: he isn't, and he wants to work powerfully through us to bring change.

BOLDNESS TO SPEAK OUT

After speaking out God's sovereignty, the disciples ask God to help them "speak [his] word with all boldness" (Acts 4:29). As we have seen, opposition to the gospel is not really a problem for God. He just uses it to further his purposes. When people are martyred, more believe through their testimony. When persecution scatters the church, the gospel spreads further and faster. The real issue is whether the message gets out there at all. That is why we must not let threats intimidate us into silence. Making people "greatly annoyed" (Acts 4:2) is enough to make my knees knock, so imagine how the disciples felt when faced with imprisonment, torture, and death. They had seen Jesus crucified, and now that same threat hung over them.

They could have tried to console themselves with the hope that "it might not happen", but of course we know that it did. Most of them were eventually martyred in various ways for speaking out about Jesus. They could have watered down the message to try to make it more palatable for everybody, but in so doing it would have lost its potency. Instead of taking either of these two false steps, they called out to God for help.

This was, and is, the best response to threats, and God answered their prayer by filling them with his Spirit. It was through being filled with the Spirit that Peter had the courage to speak to the hostile authorities in the first place (Acts 4:8)— but how did being filled with the Spirit have that effect?

Well, the only thing that casts out fear of this magnitude is love (1 John 4:18), and as they were filled with the Spirit of love (2 Timothy 1:6) the paralysing spell of fear was broken. I read a story once of a boy who kept going back into a burning building to rescue members of his family. What do you think enabled him to overcome the instinctive, inbuilt fear of fire? It was love. Love compelled him to go through the flames time and time again to rescue one person after another. Sadly he was eventually overcome by smoke and died. He gave up his life to save others which, according to Jesus' closest friend John, is right at the heart of what defines love (1 John 4:10).

As they prayed, the same Spirit that was on Jesus when he willingly went to the cross flooded the early disciples with God's love for the lost. There is nothing in this world that is a match for God's supernatural, divine love for people. It will empower us and compel us to press through any threat, intimidation, or pain to reach more precious people with the good news of Jesus Christ.

THE SUPERNATURAL SPEARHEAD

So the disciples prayer is about God's sovereignty and asking for his help to speak boldly, but they do not stop there. In order to fight an effective ground war, they need to call in supporting cover from the air, and here is where we see again the significance of supernatural healing in the proclamation of the gospel. They pray, "Stretch out your hand to heal" (Acts 4:30). Instead of looking for another strategy, they look to press forward with healing as the supernatural spearhead of gospel advance.

Our lives are important in proclaiming the gospel. The way we conduct ourselves and love one another is, of course, a witness to the truth. There is also a place for giving a reason for the hope that we have (1 Peter 3:15) and articulating the gospel message in a way that overcomes misconceptions and misunderstandings, but can you see how significant healing is here? They do not pray that God helps them love one another better or that he gives them greater intelligence to argue their case. They may have done so at other times, but here their cry is that God would heal people and perform lots of miracles. That needs to be our prayer too: "Sovereign Lord, let us preach your word with boldness and stamp it with your hallmark of healing."

God loves that sort of prayer. How do we know? Because he answered it right away. As soon as they had stopped praying, God shook the building. It's as if the launch code had just been entered into an underground missile system. The ground shakes as the rocket bursts into life and lifts off the ground. God says, "Yes! I love that prayer" and turns on the power. The Holy Spirit is poured out, and the disciples are once again propelled out of their silos to devastate the kingdom of darkness.

RESOLVE TO REACH FOR FRUIT

God wants us to reach for fruit in supernatural healing. We should never let go of this or change our strategy, but keep believing God that the fruit is there for the taking. Don't be intimidated or discouraged. Preach the gospel with signs and wonders accompanying. Will we resolve to communicate the gospel God's way, with healing as the hallmark?

What will you do with everything you have just read? Remember the blessing is not in the hearing of God's word but in the doing of it, so why not be bold and step out in the good of it? That, after all, is the second thing that the disciples did. They prayed, then they once again reached out for fruit in supernatural healing and, as we read on in Acts, it seems that they reaped quite a harvest. Let us follow their example so that we, too, might reap the harvest that we long for.

QUESTIONS

1) What is one of the scariest situations you have ever been in? Were you able to overcome your fear and if so how? What would you do next time if you were faced with the same situation?

2) In what ways are you tempted to hold back from telling people about Jesus? How can you respond in such a way that the gospel still gets out?

3) What will you do to ensure that supernatural healing plays a more prominent role in your demonstration and proclamation of the gospel?